Tracy'

Enjoy the book!

Bill Carmen

SAVING NOAH

SAVING NOAH

Love, Murder, and Kentucky Politics

by
William F. Carman

Acclaim Press
MORLEY, MISSOURI

Acclaim Press
— Your Next Great Book —

P.O. Box 238
Morley, MO 63767
(573) 472-9800
www.acclaimpress.com

Editor: Randy Baumgardner
Book & Cover Design: Rodney Atchley

ISBN: 978-1-948901-81-9 | 1-948901-81-1
Library of Congress Control Number: 2020952181

First Printing 2021
Printed in the United States of America
10 9 8 7 6 5 4 3 2 1

This publication was produced using available information.
The publisher regrets it cannot assume responsibility for errors or omissions.

Contents

"Blessed are the peacemakers,
for they shall be called the children of God."
Matthew 5:9

PROLOGUE

This is the story of Sheriff Noah Tipton and his death in 1932. It is also the story of two women. Noah's wife, Lillie, was appointed Rockcastle County Sheriff after Noah's murder. Her new job could have been honorary—a way of compensating her in a small way for her loss—but Lillie took the job seriously. Also central to this story is my mother, Wathalyne, who was affected by the loss of her grandfather, and became my window into those events.

Like a soldier returning from the pain of war, my mother never spoke of the death of Noah. The first time I heard the story was from a man who came into my office back in 1981, offering to sell me tickets to the Rotary Club pancake breakfast. Upon learning my name, he asked me if I was related to Wathalyne Carman. I told him I was her son, and he then asked me if she ever told me the story of her grandfather's death. I replied that she had not, and he then offered a narrative of a sheriff murdered by a hit-man. That, of course, piqued my interest. I subsequently asked Mom about Noah. Her eyes welled with pain, but she offered very little to add to what I had learned.

In 2003, a friend and co-worker, Mark Morgan, mentioned that he was going to the Kentucky State Archives to do some family research. I gave him Noah's name and asked him if he might poke around a bit and see what he could learn. He returned with a headline article from the *Lexington Leader* newspaper that reported Noah's death. That article whetted my appetite for more information, and I began gently questioning my mother about the events.

Over the next seven years, until Mom died in 2010, she slowly revealed the story to me. I began supplementing her story with information from other sources. By then I had retired from my long-term career and had taken a job with a non-profit conservation organization. My job took me all across Kentucky, and I started devoting some of my road time to stopping by courthouses, libraries, and newspaper offices, hoping to fill in some blanks. Mom also accompanied me to some of those destinations, places that were a part of her youth and critical to the story of Noah.

My father had died when I was thirty-one. He was a loving father and we had a very good relationship. However, I deeply miss being Dad's friend as a contemporary adult. My time with Mom allowed me to not only be her son, but her friend as well. Noah's story enabled that relationship to mature, and for that I am eternally thankful.

After Mom's death, my research hit a dead end. I had many unanswered questions. Any notion that my journey might result in a book was far-fetched. But then I met Jean Burchell.

Hunter Burchell was the man who killed Noah Tipton. I never imagined that one of Hunter's descendants, a Burchell, would be the key to my research.

On one of my trips, a chance encounter in a restaurant and several subsequent phone calls led me to Jean Burchell, who lives in northwestern Pennsylvania. Jean's late husband, Bob, was Hunter Burchell's nephew. Jean and I struck up a friendship via emails and telephone.

Jean is not only an accomplished amateur historian, but she is the de facto Burchell family genealogist. She had encountered the story of Noah's death in her own research, and she generously sent me literally everything she had about the killing—a large stack of documents, photographs, and a flash drive containing the electronic versions of the same material. At one point I suggested to her that she and

I co-author a book. She seemed honored but declined. So, Jean, thank you so much for your support and inspiring me to continue my research and to write this book.

The frustrating characteristic of researching a book like this one is that for every answer you find, another two or three questions materialize, and you dive into another rabbit hole to get the answers. For example, in researching the origins of the Tipton family, I found two similar family trees that had one important difference…whether Noah Tipton's father was or was not a Cherokee Indian. Figuring out why that discrepancy existed led me to the saga of the Trail of Tears and how that chapter in our American history affected my family.

It was a never-ending puzzle. I had to finally draw the line somewhere, document the remaining questions, and admit that it was time to walk away. This frustration was exacerbated by the fact that many records were destroyed by courthouse fires, flooded newspaper offices, and the deaths of officials whose records were discarded afterward. In this day of easy internet research, you soon come to realize that the internet only goes as far as the records that still exist.

It must be noted that this book is not a scholarly history. I attempted to stay true to the historic records I found, and to the stories told to me by family members. I have listed the sources of my information at the end of the book, but I did not utilize footnotes. I believe they are a distraction, and they would establish a scholarly standard to which I had no intention of achieving. It is my hope that the reader will view this book as creative non-fiction, a memoir, a good story, my interpretation of the records, and nothing more.

I worked on this book for nearly two decades, but my efforts really picked up steam during the COVID-19 lockdown in the early spring of 2020. As I sat at my computer, gazing out the window at empty streets, it was easy for me to empathize with Americans in the early 1930s who had lost their jobs, their bank accounts, and their retirement during the Great Depression. It was against that backdrop that Noah Tipton was killed, and experiencing a taste of those times, I believe, helped me complete this book.

The title of this book, *Saving Noah,* is similar to the title of two popular movies, *Saving Private Ryan* and *Saving Mr. Banks.* I settled on the name of this book before either movie was released. I hope that readers do not think less of the book because of the name. This book is a preservation of Noah's story. His memory and the memory of the circumstances surrounding his death should be saved. Noah's name is etched on the Kentucky Law Enforcement Memorial in Richmond. I hope this book is as much a memorial as the stone monument bearing his name.

I wish I had met Noah Tipton. By the time I was born, he had been gone for nineteen years. I believe that beyond his tough persona, under his serious, no-nonsense façade, was a man who loved his family, liked to laugh, and would have had a warm handshake. I believe we would have been friends.

SAVING NOAH

Chapter One

THE MEMORIAL

My mother was no stranger to grief. Her four last names were a testament to those that she had lost. Wathalyne Tipton Fairchild Carman Hendrick had recently lost her second husband, Bill Hendrick. Her first husband and father of her two sons, Brodie Carman, had died twenty-five years earlier. Her own father, Marvin Fairchild, had died when she was eleven from an illness that is now casually treated with a simple antibiotic. And her beloved grandfather, Noah Tipton, had died violently in the street. His death was why she was sitting on a folding chair in the green spring grass, gazing at the warm sun.

As the oldest descendant of Sheriff Noah Tipton, Mom had been invited to a ceremony hosted by the Kentucky Law Enforcement Memorial Foundation at Eastern Kentucky University. The ceremony had been organized to recognize Kentucky law enforcement officers killed in the line of duty. Noah Tipton was one of those fallen officers honored. The names of the officers killed in the line of duty had been etched on a metal plaque, and each name was read aloud, along with a brief description of the events surrounding those deaths.

Others sat on folding chairs around her...politicians, widows, orphaned children, bereaved parents, and men and women in uniform. Mom wore her Sunday best, a striking silk blouse with a turquoise scarf. Her silver hair was brushed back around her smooth olive skin and brown eyes.

She listened intently to the speakers as they solemnly described heroic men and heroic actions. There was a pause in the ceremony, and she stood as a uniformed officer presented her with a folded American flag. She sat down and held the flag against her chest like a treasure. Her mind drifted back. A tear trickled down her cheek. It could have been from the sun or the cool spring breeze, but it wasn't. She was remembering a rainy January evening that brought sorrow to her family and brought her to this place seventy-six years later.

Mt. Vernon, Kentucky is a sleepy little town nestled in the foothills of the Appalachians. It has one stoplight downtown surrounded by neat frame houses and tree-lined streets. In the winter of 1932, the dripping trees held the smoke from fireplaces, coal furnaces, and potbellied stoves like a shroud over a battlefield.

Like most small towns in Kentucky, life in Mount Vernon centered around high school sports, and wood smoke over rural Kentucky meant it was basketball season. On that Saturday evening, January 16th, as the sun dropped over the hills to the west, clouds were gathering. It began to spit rain and a promise of snow was on the breeze.

Coach Marvin Fairchild never went anywhere without his two daughters, one nine and the other seven. On this night they were going to the Mt. Vernon High School basketball game, but first, Coach had to drop off the mail at the Post Office. His wife, Dolora, wouldn't stand for a bill being paid late, and in the winter bad weather could delay the mail. So, Coach pulled his car to the curb in front of the Post Office. He left the girls in the front seat, covered by a wool blanket, giggling at the squeaking of the wipers on the windshield.

The windows began to fog, so Geraldine, the youngest, reached up and drew a stick-girl on the moist glass with her finger.

"Don't do that, Geri! Daddy will get mad."

"No, he will not, Sister!"

It seemed that Wathalyne, the oldest, was always refereeing the conflicts arising from the gentle discipline rationed out by her father and the high-spirited will of her younger sibling. As a youngster learning to talk, Geri couldn't pronounce Wathalyne, so she simply called her older sister "Sister."

Sister rubbed a circle of fog from the window. She could see her Daddy striding back across the Post Office lawn, holding his coat over his head in the mist. He opened the door and slid behind the wheel as the girls wriggled beneath the blanket.

They loved their Daddy. They loved his smile and big hands and the smell of his shaving lotion. They loved him even more than they loved their Granddaddy Noah. They sometimes called Granddaddy "Pa." He was the sheriff and he often rode a big black horse and wore a black hat. Pa smelled like leather and always brought them apples.

Coach hugged his daughters and smiled, saying, "Let's go, we're running late."

Pow-Pow

"What was that, Daddy?"

Coach quickly rolled down the window.

Pow-Pow

"What was that noise, Daddy?"

Pow

"I don't know, girls. Be still."

He let off the clutch and the car slowly moved forward. He craned his neck, looking out the window, and pulled out onto Main Street. A man darted across the street in the headlights. A woman ran down the sidewalk, clutching her purse and holding her hat on her head with one hand. People were gathering under the streetlight in front of the drugstore. Coach quickly turned the car to the curb and pulled on the emergency brake.

"Girls, you stay here." He looked at them sternly and repeated himself, turning their little heads with his hand so they looked directly into his eyes.

"Girls, you stay in the car. Do you hear me?"

"Yes," they said in unison.

He opened the door and walked quickly toward the gathering crowd. A man yelled. Others were wrestling a man to the sidewalk. In the circle of light pale faces were staring at a figure lying face-down in the street. Marvin saw the black hat lying in a puddle of rain and blood, and he knew instantly who it was.

—⁂—

The ceremony concluded. Mom stood up and walked tentatively toward the stone monument. She paused and reached for the stone, steadying herself. Her hand swept over the names until she found "Noah J. Tipton — Rockcastle County" engraved in the satin metal plaque. Her fingers explored the words, feeling the depth of their meaning, and she knew then that Noah's story would not be just a memory.

Chapter Two
JANUARY 16, 1932

Sheriff Noah Tipton had calmed down, but he was still angry. It had been an ordinary Saturday morning at the Rockcastle County Courthouse. He had arrived early and completed the ledger entries for the property tax receipts that had arrived in Friday's mail. He then stepped into the courtroom to see if Judge Tarter needed anything during a pause in the Miller Trial. It was unusual for a trial to continue on a Saturday, but this trial was unusually complicated and required more than a normal workweek to conclude. It was then that the day became anything but ordinary.

Hunter Burchell, a prison guard from the State Prison in Frankfort, had been sent to Mount Vernon to drive and guard Floyd Miller, an inmate at the prison who was to be called as a witness in the trial of his brother, Robert Miller. Both Floyd and Robert had been arrested for receiving deposits at the People's Bank of Mount Vernon after the bank had been declared insolvent. What they did with those deposits was the subject of the current trial.

But Hunter was not guarding Floyd Miller. He was simply accompanying him, like an old friend. They had been seen at restaurants, visiting acquaintances, and generally having a grand time at the taxpayer's expense. The citizens of Mount Vernon were irate, particularly those who had lost money when the bank folded. They complained to Sheriff Tipton, who in turn called the Attorney General, who then called Warden William Roach, who undoubtedly called Hunter Burchell. Despite the fact that the warden was Hunter's brother-in-law, the call from him had not been pleasant.

Hunter stormed into the courtroom, swearing, and loudly expressing his displeasure at Sheriff Tipton. Judge Tarter ordered the Sheriff to remove Burchell and to calm him down. The two men quickly walked into the hallway and into a vacant jury room next door.

Noah was a big man, well over six feet tall, and had the raw-boned build of a man who had grown up on a farm. Hunter was a small man—under five foot six inches—who had a temper sharpened by years of overcompensating for his small stature. Noah was the sheriff of Rockcastle County and this was *his* county, and *his* courthouse, and Burchell had angered *his* people. He would not be threatened or intimidated by this little man who dared to question him for doing his job.

Both men were armed, and it is easy to imagine that the slightest gesture by Burchell toward his weapon resulted in looking down the barrel of Noah's own gun. No one witnessed the encounter, but Burchell left the courthouse angry at being completely humiliated. He walked quickly to the Miller residence and spent the afternoon stewing. Encouraged by the Millers, Burchell became angrier and angrier.

Noah finished his routine office duties and decided to walk home. The afternoon air had warmed, and he was glad to be outside. The familiar streets, the houses of neighbors, and the thought of Lillie's kitchen cleared his head of the morning's unpleasantness. Before he climbed the steps onto his porch, he turned and walked across the side yard and opened the pasture gate. His horse, Blackie, nickered and shook his head. Noah took Blackie's halter and led him toward the small barn. Just inside the open door, Noah picked up a bucket, and scooped several handfuls of oats from a feed bag. He secured Blackie in the barn's only stall and poured the oats into the small feed trough.

"Yore a good'un, yes you are," he told the horse as he rubbed its neck. Noah closed the stall and turned toward the house.

Lillie looked up as Noah entered the kitchen. "Are your feet clean?"

She then noticed his stocking feet and smiled, wiping her hands on her apron. "Made you some beans and cornbread so's you can eat before the game. "

Noah bent down and kissed Lillie on her forehead. He sat down heavily at the kitchen table and sighed.

"Had to tell that prison guard you just can't do what he did in our town."

"What'd he say?"

"Not much. I don't like him a whit."

Lillie put her hand on Noah's shoulder. "You be careful. A man like that's not to be trusted."

Noah leaned over and inhaled the steam from the hot plate and smiled. "This'll do!"

He picked up a knife an began buttering the cornbread. He felt a soft nudge on his leg and peered beneath the table. His cat, Fluffy, was circling his legs, purring.

"She smells the bacon in your beans and wants some."

"That ol' cat is fat enough. Don't you dare give her table food," she said as she grabbed a dish towel. "Shoo!" She waved the towel at the cat as it slunk away toward the living room.

After lunch he shoved his chair back and exhaled, looking at his watch and said, "I'd better git."

Lillie was putting dishes in the sink when he stepped up behind her and wrapped his big arms around her waist.

"Wanna go to the game with me?"

"No," she replied, "but you cheer some for me."

Noah pulled on his shoes and slipped out the door, listening to Lillie whistle to the sound of dishes clinking in the kitchen. He turned toward downtown, knowing he would see lots of friends in town, gathering for the evening's basketball game at Mount Vernon High School. His son-in-law was the coach and the team had been doing well.

Downtown Mount Vernon was bustling, excited that the home team had a very real chance at a District Championship. The day had been unseasonably warm but there was now a chill in the air. Folks were enjoying the afternoon, shopping, eating at the Ideal Cafe, and standing in small groups on the street corners, chatting about the game, recent New Year's festivities, and offering local gossip. Some of that gossip no doubt included the Miller brothers and the trial.

Noah stopped beneath the drugstore canopy on Main to speak to his old boss, retired Sheriff John Griffin. Noah had spent several years as a deputy under Griffin, and they had a friendship forged by several close scrapes, including a gunfight that wounded both men and resulted in two dead felons.

The warm day was becoming cold and was spitting rain. Noah turned up the collar of his long overcoat and buttoned the top buttons. Griffin had already heard about Burchell's ill behavior and patted Noah on the shoulder and shook his head, offering encouragement.

A loud voice cut the air. "Sheriff Noah Tipton! You are telling people you rubbed a pistol in my face!"

Noah instantly recognized the voice. Burchell stepped forward, screaming into Noah's face. Noah could feel his hot breath and see his red eyes.

He shoved Burchell back and shouted, "Go away! I don't want to argue with you on the street."

Then he saw Burchell's gun. He heard the first shot as he reached for his own gun, but his coat was buttoned. The bullet's impact staggered him backward, and a second shot brought him to his knees. As he was falling, Burchell calmly walked up to him. As Noah Tipton lay face down, dying on the street, Hunter Burchell shot him twice more in the back of the head. It was an execution.

Sheriff Griffin immediately tackled Burchell, and several other men, including Deputy Charles Carter, who had just crossed the street, joined in. Carter had drawn his own gun when he heard the shots, and in the scuffle, Carter's gun discharged into the air. At the sound of the first shot, Deputy R.T. Abney turned and sprinted toward the courthouse to retrieve his gun, fearing an all-out gunfight. Before he could return, Burchell had been subdued and disarmed. Abney met the men halfway down the street and assisted in dragging Burchell to the jail in the courthouse.

Sheriff Noah Tipton had been gunned down in cold blood, in front of witnesses. He left a grieving widow, a daughter, two granddaughters, an extended brokenhearted family, and a shocked community. The citizens were already angry about a thief running free. They were now enraged.

John Griffin, who had taken charge of the situation minutes after the shooting, immediately arranged for Burchell to be driven to Danville, thirty miles away. Danville was a larger community with a jail and a police force willing to secure the prisoner. Had Burchell remained in Mount Vernon, Griffin feared that a lynch mob would bring swift justice. This was an open and shut case of capital murder. Griffin was confident that justice would eventually be served. He underestimated the power of Kentucky politics.

Noah's lifeless body was taken to the office of Dr. Monroe Pennington, a local family physician. He signed the death certificate and wrote "Death by gunshot" under "cause of death." Dr. Pennington performed only a perfunctory autopsy. (Note: That autopsy report has been lost. More than likely because there were multiple witnesses, the autopsy simply observed the number of entry and exit wounds and their locations on the body...two in the chest and two in the back of Noah's head. His later testimony at trial confirmed that conclusion.)

Dr. Pennington was one of the few doctors in the area and was a true family physician. He delivered most of the local babies for many years, was well-liked, and his opinion valued. He had witnessed the results of accidents, illnesses, and violence, but this sickened him.

Marvin Fairchild, Noah's son-in-law, who had left his two young daughters in his car, had been on the scene within seconds of the shooting. He immediately turned and rushed his daughters home. He broke the bad news to his wife—Noah's daughter, Dolora—and then walked to Noah's house to tell Lillie. He later said telling them about Noah's death was the hardest thing he ever had to do.

On January 17th, Noah's body was embalmed at the Cox Funeral Parlor and placed in a decorative casket. As was the custom in those days, the body was then moved to Noah's home where an all-night vigil was held. My mother, who attended the vigil, remembered peeking from under the dining room table at family and friends who arrived to pay their respects. Mom always remembered the whispers, the ticking of the grandfather clock in the hallway, and the smell of flowers. From that day forward, Mom disliked the smell of flowers.

Noah was buried at Elmwood Cemetery on Monday January 18, 1932. It was reported by several newspapers that the funeral was the largest in Mount Vernon's history. The graveside service was conducted by Rev. E.S. Gaylor, the preacher at the First Baptist Church. A local photographer snapped a photo of the service. John Griffin, who had stepped in to organize the ceremony, stood prominently in the center of the photo. John, who had been at Noah's side through thick and thin, knelt in the brown winter grass to bid his companion farewell.

Chapter Three

TROUBLING TIMES

In these days of convenience store robberies, school shootings, nightly television reruns of crime stories, cowboy movies with more gunfire than Vietnam, and many Hollywood films that glamorize violence, we have come to take murder for granted. The good guys kill the bad guys and life goes on. But, in reality, violence does not always leave a dead villain, and often the dead leave grieving widows, horrified families, and communities in shock. January 16, 1932 was a day that illustrated that reality.

1932 was a year that straddled the generations involved in both America's westward expansion and the modern era. Libby Custer, the wife of General George Armstrong Custer, was still alive and would live another year. Wyatt Earp had only been dead two years and his wife, Josephine Marcus Earp, was still alive and would live another twelve years. There were still Civil War veterans in America, and Lula Parker, the sister of Robert Leroy Parker, also known as Butch Cassidy, was still alive. She claimed that despite rumors of Butch's death in 1908 in Bolivia, Butch had visited her in 1925.

But, even with the presence of living reminders of our nation's birthing pains, America was growing up. In 1932, General Electric unveiled its new all-steel electric refrigerator. The aviatrix, Amelia Earhart, completed the first transatlantic solo flight by a woman. Pontiac rolled out its new V-8 sedan, and the Holland Company started making home air conditioning units.

In 1932, nothing in America affected the mood, politics, and day-to-day lives more than the Great Depression. The stock market crashed on October 29, 1929, resulting in business closures, personal tragedies, bank failures, and unemployment over twenty-five percent. The pain of the Depression would not begin to recede until the mid 1930s when the new President, Franklin Roosevelt, initiated the Banking Act and the New Deal, and the U.S. gave up the Gold Standard.

Imagine yourself in 1929, having a decent job, and both a checking and savings account in the local bank. Every month you put a few dollars in the stock market, limiting your investments to good, solid American companies. You were optimistic, enjoying your job, and looking forward to a modest family vacation. But then you woke up one morning and the stock market had crashed, turning your dollars into pennies. Your bank closed and you lost your checking funds and savings. And then your boss tells you that he can't afford to pay you because there are no customers. Overnight, you have nothing. Your faith in America is shaken and perhaps you are wondering how a just God could let this happen. Now, you and your family must resort to standing in a food line just to eat.

The Great Depression was exacerbated by a severe drought that extended across America's Great Plains from the early 1930s until 1940. Sometimes called the "Dust Bowl," those areas hardest hit experienced failed crops, severe soil erosion from the wind, cracked earth, dust storms, and catastrophic financial losses that were compounded by the collapse of the nation's economy.

In part due to the economic condition of the country, and the distrust of banks and big business, the period between 1932 and 1934 has been called "two years of mayhem." In 1932 a young parolee named Clyde Barrow and his girl-friend Bonnie Parker begin terrorizing the South and Midwest. Both John Dillinger and Baby Face Nelson were on a rampage. The Great Depression was choking the economy when Prohibition created a fertile environment for the likes of Al Capone and his nemesis, Elliott Ness. Joe Urschel's book, *The Year of Fear,* chronicles the 1933 manhunt for Machine Gun Kelly, an event which began with Kelly's involvement in bootlegging in 1932. Charles Lindbergh's infant son was kidnapped in 1932, an event that horrified a nation that was already hardened by daily violence in the newspapers and on the radio.

In 1931 author Stuart Lake published *Frontier Marshal.* With input from both Wyatt and Josephine Earp, Lake wrote a somewhat fictionalized account of Wyatt Earp's life in Dodge City and Tombstone. Average American citizens were barely scraping by, but they dug deep, and the book became a national best seller. They admired Earp's courage and no-nonsense toughness in the face of violent force. He became an American hero, the iconic force that had protected us from criminals.

Against this backdrop, the People's Bank of Mount Vernon failed, thanks in part to two brothers, Floyd and Robert Miller, bank employees who had accepted and re-routed deposits on an insolvent bank and used them for personal gain. They were both arrested. Floyd Miller was tried and convicted and sent to the Kentucky State Reformatory in Frankfort. Robert's trial had been scheduled. Many citizens of Mount Vernon had lost their life savings, and they were angry.

The environment in Rockcastle County was much more than just stock market trends and unemployment statistics. A perusal of the court records for the period shows a dramatic increase in arrests for chicken theft and moonshining. Prohibition had created a market for illegal whiskey. Starving families resorted to stealing poultry for the table. In 1929, a seasoned Deputy Sheriff named Noah Tipton, a man who had proven himself in both popularity and toughness in the face of danger, was elected Rockcastle County Sheriff on the Republican ticket. He was exactly what the law-abiding citizens of Mount Vernon wanted.

While Sheriff Tipton was settling into his new job in Mount Vernon, a nondescript native of Clay County, Hunter Burchell, who had been an Army Mess Sergeant and had tried farming in Shelby County, went to work for his brother-in-law who was the Warden of the Kentucky State Penitentiary in Frankfort. He moved in with Jennings, his brother, who also worked at the prison, and who owned a small bungalow on St. Clair Street at the edge of downtown Frankfort. With the oversight and support of the warden, the new prison guard also settled into his job.

Noah Tipton was a native of Harlan County. He fell in love with a spirited young girl named Lillie Helton and, despite her tender age, married her. They eventually migrated to Rockcastle County, and he dabbled in farming, but through hard work and a sharp business mind, he bought into a rock quarry business in Mount Vernon. He accumulated land in Rockcastle County and took the part-time job of Deputy Sheriff. But his native Harlan County was never far from his mind.

Harlan County, called "Bloody Harlan" in the late 1800s and early 1900s, had been the epicenter of a series of nasty feuds in the mountains near the Virginia border. Noah knew that this environment was no place to raise a family, so Noah, his new wife Lillie Helton, and Lillie's whole family picked up and moved away. The Helton's settled in Paint Lick, and Noah and Lillie settled in just a few miles away in Roundstone.

Hunter Burchell had been pushed out of Clay County by his father, who, concerned about having young sons exposed to the violence of the Clay County feuds, forced all of his boys to join the Army as World War I broke out. Imagine a father thinking that his children would be safer at war rather than at home amidst the violence of the feuds.

The paths of these two men were destined to cross in January of 1932, in an event that would forever change the lives of those they loved.

Chapter Four

MT. VERNON, KENTUCKY

My earliest memories of Mt. Vernon are the sounds of a train rumbling along the tracks that form the town's edge. The sound would wake me in the dark as I slept in the upstairs bedroom of my grandmother's house on Williams Street. The other distinct memory that I hold is the sight and smell of woodsmoke on the bleak winter landscape, probably because, as a child, the most frequent visits I made to Mt. Vernon were with my family during Thanksgiving and Christmas.

Mt. Vernon is the county seat of Rockcastle County. The county is roughly three hundred square miles in size, and includes two other small towns, Brodhead to the north and Livingston to the south. There are dozens of tiny crossroads communities, most not large enough to warrant their own post offices, with names like Wellhope, Orlando, Wildie, and Burr. In 1932, the population of the whole county was around 15,000 inhabitants.

Rockcastle County was named for the Rockcastle River, which was in turn named for the large rock formations common in the Kentucky's mountains. It was first called Castle Rock and re-named when it formally became Rockcastle County in 1810. The little pioneer village of Mt. Vernon had first been named Langford Station, after an early pioneer, Stephen Langford, who settled there near a bubbling spring called Spout Springs. He was an important early pioneer who built a portion of the Wilderness Road.

Mt. Vernon was re-named for George Washington's home in 1811. It had been one of the early settlements along both the Wilderness Road and Boone Trace, early paths taken by settlers traveling through the Cumberland Gap toward the rich game lands and fertile farming opportunities to the north in the Bluegrass region of Kentucky.

Other Kentucky towns play a role in the story of Noah and Lillie Tipton. About forty miles southeast of Mt. Vernon lies the town of Manchester, the home of Hunter Burchell. Eighty miles to the northwest of Mt. Vernon is Frankfort, Kentucky's capital, and in 1932 the home of the Kentucky State Reformatory, where Hunter Burchell worked. He lived near the prison on St. Clair Street. Twenty-five miles west of Mt. Vernon is Somerset, the county seat of Pulaski County. The trial of Hunter Burchell was held in the Pulaski County Courthouse in downtown Somerset. Twenty-five miles north of Mt. Vernon is Danville and the Boyle County Jail, where Burchell was sent immediately after Noah Tipton's murder. Today, Interstate 75 (I-75) and the wide, smooth state highways make travel between these towns fast in comparison to the year 1932, when driving to any of these communities was an adventure.

Rockcastle County has been a Republican stronghold for years. The only period when the citizens of Rockcastle County did not vote Republican in local and national elections was during post-Civil War Reconstruction between 1868 through 1880. In all other elections and in all other years, Mt. Vernon and Rockcastle County residents have been loyal members of the Republican Party and have voted accordingly. This fact played heavily into the events that followed the murder of Sheriff Noah Tipton.

The office of County Sheriff has its roots in old England. The story of Robin Hood and the Sheriff of Nottingham is one we all have heard. Generally, the Sheriff is the chief law enforcement officer of a jurisdiction, which is usually the county. However, in Kentucky, we have several law enforcement agencies that have overlapping jurisdictions. In larger communities, the Police Chief is responsible for law enforcement within the city limits. Lexington is an exception, because it is an Urban-County Government, and the Police Chief handles law enforcement to the county line. In Lexington, there is a sheriff's department whose primary responsibility is serving court orders and collecting property taxes. Other law enforcement offices include the State Police (or commonly called the Highway Patrol), an organization that has police powers statewide, handles traffic enforcement, and is often called into rural communities where additional manpower and expertise is needed. United States Marshals are generally responsible for tracking down felons that have fled jail or pending legal action, and often work closely with local law enforcement. The Drug Enforcement Administration, or DEA, is responsible for handling enforcement pertaining to illegal narcotics distribution. Homeland Security is responsible primarily for neutralizing terrorist threats. In border states, such as Texas, the U.S. Border Patrol has enforcement duties, but of course, not in Kentucky.

Kentucky Conservation Officers, employed by the Kentucky Department of Fish and Wildlife Resources, are responsible for enforcing fish and game regulation, but they also are involved in investigating related mishaps and deaths from boating accidents, hunting accidents, and drownings. The Alcohol, Tobacco, and Firearms (ATF) branch of federal law enforcement handles issues like smuggling liquor, cigarettes, and investigating bombings. The U.S. Treasury and the Federal Bureau of Investigation both enforce varying federal laws in the states as well. And, the railroads have their own agents responsible for the security of the trains and tracks. All of these law enforcement offices cooperate in overlapping jurisdictional issues.

However, in 1932, in Mt. Vernon, Kentucky, law enforcement was much less complicated. The County Sheriff was the primary law enforcement officer. Mt. Vernon did (and still does) have a modest police department that handled traffic, vandalism, and petty crime inside the small city limits, but up into the 1950s the police officers did not even have drivers' licenses. From time to time, the U.S. Treasury "revenue agents" were called in to handle moonshining or bootlegging violations, but most of the time the County Sheriff enforced those laws as well.

Mt. Vernon's central business district is only two blocks long. Today, as in many American small towns, some of the storefronts are vacant due to competition from box stores and mail order retailers. In 1932, there was a small train depot next to the tracks on the west end of downtown. On the south side of Main Street sat the Miller residence, a movie theater, several retail shops and the People's Bank. The Rockcastle County Courthouse loomed large at the east end of Main. Across from the courthouse was the small Post Office, the Ideal Café, Cox's Drugstore, and several other retail shops. Elmwood Cemetery lies on a green hillside overlooking the east end of Main Street. In the small valley below the Elmwood Cemetery and adjacent to Spring Street is Spout Springs, where early pioneers had access to clean water for drinking and commerce. A hardware store stood at the corner of Williams and Main, three blocks from Downtown.

The largest business in town, the rock quarry, lies two blocks further west and two blocks south along the railroad at the end of Quarry Street. Connecting Quarry Street and Williams is Poplar Street. Sheriff Noah Tipton and his wife, Lillie lived in a small bungalow on a two-acre tract at the corner of Poplar and Quarry.

Mt. Vernon High School sat across the railroad tracks and four blocks north and three blocks west of downtown. In 1932, the Mt. Vernon High School basketball team, coached by Noah Tipton's son-in-law, Marvin Fairchild, would win the district title. Noah did not live to see the Mt. Vernon Red Devils win the championship game.

On the north side of Main, Cox's Drugstore inhabited the left side of the brick Bryant Building that had been built seven years earlier. A small alcove sheltered the doors to each side of the building. Just to the left of the alcove, in front of the large drugstore window, a steel grate covers a utility vault. In 1932, small children entering the drugstore would regularly jump up and down on the grate, enjoying the hollow sound echoing into the shaft. The alcove and grate are still there today. It was into that alcove that Noah Tipton and John Griffin had stepped to avoid the evening rain on January 16, 1932, when Hunter Burchell approached.

Chapter Five

NOAH AND LILLIE

Piecing together the quilt of someone's life is difficult, particularly if you don't know them. I never met Noah Tipton, but I did know Lillie, but only as a child can know an elder, not in a thoughtful way, but in fleeting glimpses. Trying to get to really know Lillie, forty-five years after her death, and Noah, eighty-eight years after his murder, is like sewing together a patchwork of information from my own memories, genealogy research, old newspapers, photo albums, and family stories.

So, what was Noah Tipton like? What was his personality? I inherited nice portraits of Noah and Lillie that were done shortly before Noah's death. They are photographs that were "colorized." The photographer took black and white photos, developed the film and added color to the final printed pictures.

In gazing at the photo of Noah, it is easy to imagine his personality. From all accounts, he was a loving husband, father, and grandfather. That tenderness is visible in his countenance. But, Noah was also known as a tough man who little patience for foolishness. That is also visible. I imagine that his voice was firm, and his words spare.

In the picture of Noah, he had several writing pens in his breast pocket. Noah had little formal education, but he was an accomplished businessman, and in the position of Sheriff, he had to juggle the duties of law enforcement, tax collection, running an office, and pleasing the sitting members of Rockcastle County fiscal court. He owned several properties around town and had to maintain the interests of the businesses in which he partnered. And of course, he had to please the citizens of Rockcastle County who elected him. The pens in his jacket pocket are emblematic of an organized individual.

Until I was nearly grown, I only knew Lillie as "Mamaw". She was a short, round-faced woman who smelled like a warm kitchen. My most distinct memory of her was seeing her sitting, clipping newspaper stories of crime and violence, shaking her head, and clucking in disapproval. Little did I know that this woman was a courageous widow and brave peace officer in her own right.

Lillie Mae Helton Tipton was born on May 25, 1888, in Harlan County, Kentucky, the third child of John Shade Helton and Jerusha Ledford Helton. Her family would later swell to eight children. They lived in a wood frame farmhouse surrounded by wooded hillsides on the Lower Martin's Fork.

As was a common practice in the early twentieth century in rural Appalachia, Lillie married early. Not much is known about her courtship with the tall, good-looking Noah Tipton, also a Harlan County native, but they married in 1903 when she was fifteen. He was twenty-one. They may have met at the local feed store, or in church, at a barn dance, or maybe her father had dealings with Noah. Back in 1903, farmers and neighbors shared equipment, food, planting knowledge, and meals.

Noah was also born in Harlan County on August 16, 1882, the seventh child of Andrew "John Jack" Tipton and Sarah Jane Lee Tipton. The genealogy before John Jack takes an interesting twist. One set of records indicates that John Jack was born in North Carolina, his parents were Jonathon and Sally Tipton and he had a sister, Martha Patsey, who was twenty years his senior. In reviewing birth and death dates, it is possible that is true, but perhaps unlikely, as Jonathon would have been in his sixties when John Jack was born. In this narrative, Martha Patsey brought her much younger infant brother to Harlan County in 1837. Another line of the potential family tree portrays John Jack as full-blooded Cherokee Indian, who had been born in Yancey County, North Carolina and was adopted as a child by Martha Patsey Tipton, before they moved to Harlan County (he would later name one of his daughters Martha Patsey). Martha Patsey married Samuel Hensley, but John Jack kept Martha's maiden name. Research indicates that Martha Patsey always claimed that John Jack was a Cherokee and her adopted son. If true, the circumstances surrounding the adoption and journey from North Carolina to Kentucky are unknown, but it is easy to visualize the hardships endured by a single white woman with an Indian child, journeying from the mountains of North Carolina to Kentucky in the late 1830s. Did they travel on foot, by wagon, horseback, train, or in a stagecoach?

Records also hint at a rumor that John Jack was Martha's illegitimate son, the product of an affair with a Cherokee man. John Jack's father could have died before he and Martha could marry. No known photographs of John Jack exist, so we do not know if he had any physical traits of a child of mixed blood. These rumors, however, were predictable. A white woman moves to a different state with an Indian child. Some folks just think the worst. For the sake of this writing, we'll take Martha Patsey at her word.

Many Americans, including some politicians, claim to have Indian ancestry. Many do, and many only claim to be Native American to gain advantages and attention. Our "melting pot" did include Indians who intermarried with Americans of European and African heritage. Some Americans, whose families came from Appalachia, even claim a mixture of Mediterranean, African, and Indian origins, and call themselves Melungeons. Why would we claim Indian heritage, even if the Indian blood is so diluted over the generations that it barely exists?

Since truly free-roaming Indians and their cultures were exterminated by the 1890s, America's sympathies and collective conscience have grown more positive in favor of Native Americans. The atrocities committed by Indians were forgotten, and recognizing the atrocities committed by whites became common in popular culture. From Dee Brown's book, *Bury My Heart at Wounded Knee*, to movies like *Little Big Man* and *Dances With Wolves*, we have, perhaps rightly, sympathized with the plight of the Indians. James Fenimore Cooper's 1826 book, *The Last of the Mohicans*, may have been the first to illustrate the concept of the "Noble Savage" in American literature.

The common myth is that Indians have a unique, symbiotic sense of the world around them, particularly the natural environment. Indians can track game, hear woods sounds undetectable by whites, communicate with animals, and move invisibly in the forest. They only kill as much wild game as they can eat. They are the original wildlife conservationists. Of course, this myth is a caricature. Many Indians, as well as many whites, do exhibit these talents and traits, but most do not. They are now a product of either complete assimilation into American society, or the product of reservations with less than desirable conditions.

The condition of Indian reservations, or at least the physical infrastructure, has improved over the past few years due to an influx of revenue from oil drilling, mining, and casinos on Indian land. But, the reservations still have a lot of room for improvement. It is difficult to reverse a hundred years of neglect.

Growing up, I was not immune from the desire to be part Indian. My mother was very dark skinned, with brown eyes and black hair. People often thought she was Hispanic. I inherited those traits, and in the summers of my childhood, when I rarely wore a shirt, I looked like an Indian. I loved the woods, and spent my youth wandering the Kentucky forests in search of small game I could harvest with my bow and arrows.

As an adult, when I stumbled upon the term "Melungeon," I immediately did some research and discovered several sources that list of some of the common Melungeon surnames contained names from my heritage. I was sold. I *had* to be part Indian. I mentioned this to a hunting buddy, and from that point on he teased me constantly about being a Melungeon chieftain, and that the totem of my tribe was the hubcap.

So, during my research for this book, when I discovered that Noah Tipton's father, my great-great-grandfather, may have been a Cherokee, I felt vindicated. However, upon further consideration, I was conflicted. John Jack Tipton's birth date coincides with the beginning of the Cherokee Trail of Tears, a genocidal tragedy that began with the Indian Removal Act of 1830, and included the forced march of thousands of Cherokee from North Carolina to Oklahoma, and a confiscation of their Appalachian lands. Many of those Indians died along the way. Could John Jack's adoption by Martha Tipton, and their subsequent journey from North Carolina to Harlan County be related to the Trail of Tears?

John Jack's adoption could have been straightforward, the result of a mother and father who died. But, it is easy to imagine a Cherokee mother giving away her infant son to a white woman, anticipating the perils awaiting her on the Trail of Tears, and hoping her son would have a better life. In recent years Indian adoptions into white families have become quite controversial, and except in rare circumstances, are not permitted. Preserving native cultures is a priority, and adoption by whites could lead to the loss of the Indian culture. I am sympathetic to this argument.

The Indian Removal Act of 1830 led to the forced relocation of native peoples from their land in the southeastern

U.S. to lands west of the Mississippi River, primarily in Oklahoma. These new lands were to become known as Indian Territory. The Cherokee were not the only Indians relocated. The Choctaw were moved in 1831, the Seminole in 1832, the Creek in 1834, and the Chickasaw in 1837. In 1837, the year that John Jack was born, the Cherokee were forced into internment camps in East Tennessee and a forced march began in November of 1838. Over 16,000 Cherokee were relocated, and one-third died along the trail. Twenty-five million acres of Indian land were confiscated and sold (and some granted) to primarily white Americans who needed land for agriculture and industry. The major sponsor of this whole program was President Andrew Jackson. He was vocally opposed by a congressman from Tennessee named David Crockett.

Crockett's opposition led to a failed reelection bid, and his move to Texas to find his fortune amidst a revolution by the Texians to separate from Mexico and form a new republic. Davy Crockett was killed at the Alamo Mission in San Antonio when it was overrun by a large army of Mexican soldiers led by General Santa Anna in 1836.

As of this writing, no record of John Jack's adoption has been found. The circumstances surrounding it may never be known. And, to know for sure that John Jack was an Indian, I would need a DNA test.

So, I ordered one of those spit-in-a-vial kits, I spit in the vial and sent it off. After about a month, I received an email notification of the results. Based on the contents of that saliva I submitted, my origins are 39% from Scotland, 28% from England and Northwestern Europe, 12% Wales, 8% Norway, 7% Ireland, and 6% Sweden. I scrolled to the bottom of the page, hoping there was more. There wasn't. I added up the percentages, and they totaled 100%. How could this be? I was crestfallen.

Either Martha Tipton was, as one family tree indicates, John Jack's sister, or she had an illegitimate son by a white man, not an Indian. Or possibly, John Jack *was* adopted, but his parents were white. We'll never know for sure.

The records indicate that Martha had claimed John Jack was an Indian. Why would she do that? In the mid 1800's Indians were not particularly well thought-of. We have no photographs of John Jack, but maybe he was dark-complected, like me and my Mom. Maybe Martha said it in jest, because of his complexion. Or maybe she didn't say it at all. One hundred-fifty years is plenty of time for rumors to become assumed fact.

It is my hope that the reader will forgive my somewhat irrelevant foray into the history of the Trail of Tears and the American Indian. While I now know that being Indian is not part of my biological history, the experience of the Indian culture is one I appreciate and with which I empathize.

What we do know is that John Jack Tipton grew up in Harlan County, Kentucky, married, and had ten children. One of them was Noah Tipton. By all accounts, John Jack had a good life.

John Jack's wife, Sarah, died on August 10, 1890. John Jack died exactly one month later. The cause of their deaths is unknown. If she was taken by illness, he could have fallen prey to the same disease. However, it is possible that he simply died a month later from grief and complications from heartbreak.

Noah was only ten years old when his parents died. At the time, four of Noah's siblings, Rachel, William, George, and Stephen, were young adults. Presumably, he was cared for by one or more of his brothers and sisters. Little is known about Noah's life before he met Lillie Helton.

As was the custom, Noah and Lillie married after a short courtship. The ceremony was conducted by County Magistrate TB Irvin. Witnesses were William Ledford and P. Hensley. William was probably Lillie's uncle and Mr. Hensley was perhaps a friend. Noah's mother, Patsey, had married

Samuel Hensley and Noah's sister, Jane, married a Hensley, so it is possible that this witness to the ceremony was Noah's brother-in-law. It must be noted that Noah's father, John Jack, is buried in the Hensley Cemetery near Harlan, so a strong connection between the Hensley's and Tipton's surely existed.

The roles of husband and wife were very traditional for the new Tipton family. Lillie was only fifteen when they married. She was soon expecting, had little formal education by today's standards, and must have relied almost exclusively on Noah's ability to be a bread winner. He was truly her protector. He was twenty-one when they married, was a big, confident, hard-working young man, and was well-liked. He had a good head for business and he soon realized that his future in Harlan County was limited.

Harlan County is primarily mountainous country, with tillable land confined only to creek bottoms. Sometime around the time of Noah and Lillie's marriage, her parents moved the whole clan to land more suitable for farming, near Paint Lick in Garrard County. Noah's sister, Jane Hensley, died in 1918 in Paint Lick, so it appears as though the move there included some of the extended family as well. It is also likely that the Helton family relocation to Paint Lick was to be nearer Lillie's mother's family, the Ledford's. The old Paint Lick Cemetery is full of both Hensley's and Ledford's, and many of the stones are worn and the details illegible. Records indicate that Noah and Lillie's only child, Dolora, was born in Madison County at Paint Lick, shortly after that move. Noah and Lillie, with their new baby, soon moved to Roundstone, about six miles away in Rockcastle County.

The distance between Paint Lick and Roundstone today, if one is traveling on improved highways, is approximately twenty minutes if one drives to Berea on Highway 21 along Paint Lick Creek, and then drives south toward Roundstone on U.S. 25. Back in the early 1900s the shortest distance between the two crossroad communities would have been along unimproved roads that followed White Oak Creek and Copper Creek. While more direct, that trip would have taken several hours.

Paint Lick, Kentucky, has a tiny central business district made up of a half-dozen brick and stone store fronts, including a hardware store, a bank, a diner, a gift shop, and some offices. Several of the building facades have inset stones with the dates of the buildings inscribed. Most are around 1900. Paint Lick Creek, a picturesque stream no more than thirty feet wide, runs right through the little town and snakes its way out through the adjacent farmland where it provides sustenance for deer, waterfowl, and cattle.

The Helton home was situated on a hillside just a few minutes outside of Paint Lick. The view from the home to the north is a rolling green panorama of lush hilltops and timbered bottoms. The view to the south is similar, but in the distance the mountains form a backdrop. The Helton clan undoubtedly appreciated the fertile land, but also appreciated the reminder that their mountain origins were within reach.

That house still exists, albeit in a modified form. A gable has been added on the left quarter of the house, and one window has been covered. But the bones of the home are intact and have been enjoyed for a century by another family.

The move to Paint Lick may have also been rooted in the desire to flee the violence of Harlan County. Known as "Bloody Harlan" from the late 1880's, the county had experienced a protracted feud that had left many widows and grieving, angry families. By 1900, the feud was winding down, but residents no doubt felt that bloodshed could erupt again with little provocation. Understandably, the Helton family may have had enough, and Paint Lick perhaps offered both better farmland, family ties, and a more peaceful life.

Shortly after the Helton family moved to Paint Lick, Noah and Lillie moved to Roundstone. Very little of Roundstone still exists. The construction of I-75 and the widening of U.S. 25 have all but obliterated the tiny crossroads in northern Rockcastle County. The bottomland is tillable, but the hillsides are reminiscent of the hills of Harlan County. Farming there was probably not much more than a subsistence affair, and to get ahead, a farmer would need other sources of income. Roundstone was just a short drive from Mt Vernon, and Noah began dabbling in business ventures there.

Not much is known about the Tipton family life between 1904 and 1930. A 1915 Draft Registration document lists Noah's home as Conway, but that may have been the nearest post office to Roundstone, just to the south. Sketchy records indicate that Noah was a farmer, but that he eventually bought into the Sparks Lumber Yard and a rock quarry in Mount Vernon. The 1920 census indicates that Noah was still farming, but the 1930 census listed him as Sheriff. According to the *Stanford Interior Journal*, Noah was nominated on the Republican ticket as a candidate for Sheriff in August of 1929. He was probably elected in 1929 to a four-year term. We do know that he had previously served as a Deputy Sheriff under Sheriff John C. Griffin, and a 1927 newspaper article about the two men confirms that fact.

Noah and Lillie eventually moved into the community of Mount Vernon. They purchased a small bungalow at the corner of Poplar Street and Quarry Street, within walking distance of both the Rock Quarry and the Mount Vernon central business district. The house sat on about two acres of land that included a small barn, in which Noah kept his black horse in inclement weather. Noah often rode his horse to work at the Rockcastle County Courthouse, but he kept it primarily to be able to access remote areas of the county on roads that were little more than goat paths. It was his version of today's four- wheel drive SUV's.

By all accounts, Lillie was a good wife and devoted mother. Their family became a pillar of their small community. Her daughter, Dolora, met her future husband, Marvin, at Berea College, and they married and moved into a home two blocks away, on Williams Street. Marvin was a teacher and basketball coach. He and Dolora had two daughters, Wathalyne and Geraldine. Both of the little girls were often fixtures in the Tipton house, and loved playing with Noah and Lillie's cat, Fluffy. Wathalyne was my mother.

Because Lillie had married so early in life, she and her daughter were only sixteen years apart. They were close enough in age that their families were particularly close, more akin to being contemporaries.

And so went life in a small town. While Rockcastle County had its share of violence and trouble, Mount Vernon had very little. Noah's jurisdiction, from the standpoint of law enforcement, was primarily out in the county, an area of around three-hundred square miles that included small crossroad settlements like Livingston and Brodhead. His job involved collecting property taxes and serving arrest warrants for things like moonshining and chicken theft.

From time to time, the Sheriff and deputies had to venture into the hills and hollers of Rockcastle County to enforce the law, and most of those forays were unremarkable. A 1928 article in the Stanford Interior Journal describes Sheriff John Griffin and Deputy Noah Tipton taking two teenagers to the Greendale Reform School for blocking the railroad tracks at Roundstone Station. Another article in the *Interior Journal* in 1930 describes an incident where Noah and his two deputies, Abney and Carter, captured a moonshine still near Skaggs Creek with no resistance from the moonshiner.

It must be noted that Mount Vernon did have a town police force, made up of Chief Walter Sowder, and one deputy. Sowder was responsible for keeping the peace in an already peaceful community. One newspaper account indicates that he was also present and witnessed Noah's murder, but little else is known about him, and he played little if any role in the story of Noah Tipton. To illustrate the limits of the Mt. Vernon Police Department, it has been said that well into the 1950s, the two police officers, while dedicated and hard-working, did not have drivers' licenses.

As a Deputy Sheriff, Noah and Sheriff Griffin did encounter one bad scrape when they tried to arrest a band of moonshiners who chose to fight rather than go to jail. Both Noah and Griffin were wounded and two of the moonshiners were killed. However, that type of incident was very unusual. This incident is discussed in further detail in Chapter 6 of this book.

But generally, life in Mount Vernon was peaceful. Folks enjoyed Thanksgiving and Christmas with their families, attended high school basketball games, and braced for another winter in the Appalachian foothills. That peace was shattered on the night of January 16, 1932, when Hunter Burchell killed Noah Tipton.

Chapter Six

THE 1927 GUNFIGHT

Noah Tipton had faced gunfire before his murder in January of 1932. Over four years earlier, he proved his mettle in an event that nearly cost him his life and may have affected the outcome of his conflict with Hunter Burchell.

The National Prohibition Act, known as the Volstead Act, was approved by Congress as the 18th Amendment to the U.S. Constitution in October 1919. It became law in January of 1920. This controversial act prohibited the sale and consumption of alcoholic beverages. The enactment of this law spawned the clandestine, but lucrative, industries of manufacturing illegal whiskey, transporting the whiskey, selling the whiskey, and consuming it. It also brought into the public spotlight characters like Chicago's Al Capone, who profited greatly from Prohibition. Small-scale manufacturing was called moonshining. Transporting the goods was called bootlegging, and the business of selling and consuming was often done in underground bars called "speakeasies."

Moonshine whiskey was manufactured in hidden distilleries, called stills, before, during, and after Prohibition, primarily to avoid the taxes and other federal regulations on whiskey. Stills were constructed out of repurposed sheet metal and copper and hidden in remote or secret places near springs and small streams where clean water was available. Most moonshine used a fermented mixture of shelled corn, sugar, and yeast, called mash, which was distilled onsite to produce the alcohol, and poured into canning jars for distribution.

Before Prohibition, bootlegging was the business of transporting whiskey into jurisdictions where the sale was illegal, such as "dry" counties. After Prohibition became law, all transportation of whiskey was illegal. That illicit transportation was carried out in flatbed trucks, on pack animals, on horse drawn wagons with false bottoms and even smuggled onto trains. The most common method of transportation, however, was to load the liquor into automobiles that had been modified to go faster than cars driven by law enforcement. Modifying those cars became a cottage industry in and of itself, which led to southern stock car racing, and eventually NASCAR.

In the fall of 1927, the nation was in the throes of Prohibition. Rural Appalachia was a perfect place to produce moonshine, and the sweet aroma of bubbling mash drifted on the mountain breezes of Rockcastle County. On Tuesday, November 15th, Sheriff John Griffin received a tip that a gang of moonshiners would be transporting a load of illegal liquor to Mullins Station, probably to smuggle the moonshine aboard a Louisville and Nashville Railroad car.

I visited Mullins Station in the early spring, just as lavender cascades of redbuds painted the hills. The small streams were full of babbling clear water that seeped from the limestone cliffs lining the hollows. My mission was to locate both the ruins of the Mullins Station depot and possibly one of the caves rumored to have sheltered moonshine stills during Prohibition. About five miles southeast of Mt. Vernon as the crow flies, but closer to seven miles on crooked gravel roads, lies the ruins of Mullins Station. In a valley on the banks of Roundstone Creek and next to the railroad is a rocky clearing where coal, limestone gravel, and on occasion, saltpeter were loaded onto trains. On the far side of the clearing there are three large portals into the mountain where the minerals were extracted.

Mullins Station was an early pioneer community. Often called "stations", these communities sometimes grew and became towns and even cities. There are a few homes still standing a short distance from the old train depot site, but as the mineral extraction business waned, and as nearby Mt. Vernon grew, Mullins Station became a rural outpost.

The area is honeycombed with caves. Just a short distance north along the railroad from Mullins Station is a wide spot in the gravel road where a dirt trail leads down through the woods about a quarter mile to one of the many openings to the cave system. A beautiful little stream rushes through the rhododendron and mountain laurel before plunging into the mouth of the cave. The caves no doubt concealed many moonshine stills over the years.

Sheriff John Griffin, accompanied by Deputy Noah Tipton, and Cam Mullins, an agent for the railroad who had also been the Sheriff ten years earlier, left Mt. Vernon at around seven that evening, their car straining to climb the big U.S. 25 hill out of downtown. It was a cool November night, and they shivered, more out of anticipation of their mission than the cold. A mile out of town they topped the ridge and sped down toward the railroad and the gravel turnoff toward Mullins Station.

After turning away from the blacktop, the road was rough. The car's headlights bounced across the forest ahead and the guns they had stowed in the back seat rattled. John slowed the car to a crawl, not knowing exactly where they might encounter the bootleggers. The car crossed the railroad three times and they knew that the old train depot lay just ahead. Sheriff Griffin pulled the car to the right side of the road and cut the engine. Both Griffin and Deputy Tipton rolled down the car windows to listen. The car engine ticked, and Roundstone Creek gurgled over smooth rocks in the ravine below. In the darkness the men whispered small talk about their families and the upcoming holidays.

The sound of a distant engine grew louder. It stopped, and the three men could hear doors being shut and men talking. John, Noah, and Cam slowly opened the doors of John's car. They reached into the back to retrieve their weapons, and gently closed the car doors. They patted their sides to ensure their revolvers were secure, and they crept forward, staying in the grass at the side of the road to avoid crunching the gravel. Soon they could make out the outline of a flatbed truck and four men. They could see glowing cigarettes and hear voices as the men carried boxes toward a train car parked on the tracks next to the road.

John Griffin held up his hand to stop Noah and Cam. He raised his lever-action 30-30 and jacked a shell into the chamber with a loud ratcheting. The bootleggers froze in their tracks.

"Boys, this is Sheriff John Griffin. We have you covered. Set your boxes down and put your hands up. Cam, turn on the headlights of that truck. Boys, line up in the light so's we can see you."

Cam stepped forward, reached into the truck, and flipped on the headlights.

The four men shuffled toward the front of the truck, holding their hands over their eyes to shield them from the headlights. Covering them with their weapons, the three officers approached the men. John held up his badge, and it reflected the light.

"We're going to search you fellers. Don't make any sudden moves. Keep them hands up."

Cam and Noah stepped forward and Noah pulled aside one man's coat. He felt the handle of a pistol. The man quickly grabbed Noah's arm with his left hand and jerked the gun from under his coat with his right hand. He tried to get the gun up, but Noah shoved him and the gun went off, shooting a hole through Noah's left palm. The man fell backwards, still pointing his gun. Noah raised his revolver and shot the man in the chest.

Gunfire erupted and echoed through the hills. All of the men were firing simultaneously. John Griffin went down with a shot though his side. A bullet grazed Noah over his left eye, and blood poured across his face, temporarily blinding him. He dropped to one knee, wiped his face with his sleeve and kept firing at the muzzle flashes in the dark. Cam had ducked behind the truck and was trying to aim and fire over the truck's cab.

The battle lasted less than a minute and ended as abruptly as it started when the guns were empty. Two of the bootleggers lay dead in the dust. Both Noah and John were wounded, but after examining each other, they concluded they would live. The other two bootleggers had fled. Cam was unhurt, but all three men were shaken. John sent Cam for help and as he ran around the bend in the road toward John's car, he was muttering "Lordy, Lordy."

Both John and Noah sat down in the middle of the road. They were quiet. A dog barked from a far-off hillside. Mist from the creek rose and descended on them, swirling in the truck's headlights. John looked at Noah and shook his head.

"Ain't this something?" he stated, wincing at the pain in his side.

Noah was grasping a handkerchief against his brow with one hand to slow the bleeding while he clinched his other dripping fist.

"Ain't this something?" he replied.

The *Stanford Interior Journal* reported that Sheriff Griffin flashed his badge and ordered the moonshiners to surrender. One of the moonshiners pulled his pistol and, as the paper stated, "the shooting got underway."

Lillie later told family members that Noah thought he had killed both moonshiners. In 1932, John Griffin told newspaper reporters that Noah, despite being shot twice, had been the officer who fired the shots that killed them.

The Sheriff and his Deputy survived their injuries. Lillie's letter of May 13, 1932 to Governor Laffoon referred to the Grand Jury examining this incident three times and clearing Noah of any wrongdoing. No records of those Grand Jury hearings exist today, probably because no indictments were handed down. Why the matter was heard three times is unknown, but she may have referred to the grand jury examining John's actions, Noah's actions, and Cam's actions separately.

The incident cemented the friendship between John and Noah. John now knew he could count on his friend as a reliable hand in a pinch. The incident also instilled in Noah the seriousness of using deadly force. He hoped to never use it again.

The gunfight also affected Lillie. She nursed Noah back to health, but a sense of dread hung over everyday affairs. She often worried that when he walked out the door, he might not return.

As time went by, Noah's wounds healed. He was elected Sheriff, and Lillie's dread diminished. He now spent more time in the office, assigning tasks to his deputies, appearing before the Fiscal Court, and serving as the tax collector for the county. Lillie had no idea that when her son-in-law, Marvin Fairchild, knocked on her door that rainy January night four years after the Mullins Station gunfight, her worst fears would come to pass.

The *Stanford Interior Journal* story also stated that Noah had been shot in his left hand and in the head. A colorized portrait of Noah, completed shortly before his death, clearly shows a scar over his left eye. That scar is possibly a result of the 1927 gunfight. The wound to Noah's hand may have affected his use of that hand, which could have made it difficult to quickly unbutton his coat on the evening of January

16, 1932. That conjecture is more fully discussed in Chapter 8 of this book.

In 1935, three years after Noah's death, his daughter, Dolora, lost her husband, Coach Marvin Fairchild, to an infection that would today be casually treated with antibiotics. Several years later she was remarried to Bentley Mullins, the son of Cam Mullins, who had accompanied John Griffin and Noah Tipton to Mullins Station the night of the gunfight. Dolora and Bentley are buried together just a few feet from the graves of Noah and Lillie in the Elmwood Cemetery in Mt. Vernon.

Chapter Seven

HUNTER BURCHELL

William Hunter Burchell was born on November 17, 1894, in Manchester, Kentucky. He was raised on the family farm along with his nine siblings. His parents were Dr. Joseph Burchell and Sophia Garrard Burchell. Sophia was the daughter of Brigadier General T.T. Garrard and descendant of James Garrard, the first elected governor of Kentucky.

Dr. Burchell was a prominent Clay County citizen. He and his family resided on a large tract of land just northwest of Manchester called Greenbriar. The large brick home sat on a hill overlooking the road to Manchester (now Highway 638). That home no longer exists. Much of the land was eventually deeded to the city for a park and cemetery. Behind the public cemetery is the Burchell family cemetery, where Dr. Burchell, Sophia, Hunter, and his wife Ethel are buried.

As a young adult, Hunter worked as a farm laborer, and when World War I erupted all five of the Burchell sons, encouraged by their father who was worried about their violent Clay County surroundings, volunteered for military service. Hunter and his brother, Jennings, both were in the Meuse-Argonne offensive. Hunter served as a Mess Sergeant in Company A of the Second Regiment of the Kentucky National Guard. He was assigned to the HQ CO 305 Infantry in France.

World War I's Meuse-Argonne Offensive lasted forty-seven days, from September 26, 1918 until armistice on November 11, 1918. It involved 1.2 million American troops, and was the second deadliest battle in U.S. history with over 350,000 casualties, including over 26,000 American dead. During the first three hours of the offensive, the Allies expended more ammunition than both sides fired during the whole American Civil War. This was the battle that defeated the Germans and ended World War I.

Because the offensive was large in scale and complexity, many U.S. troops were involved in support roles, such as supply and mess. This is not to diminish their courage or commitment, but it is possible that Sgt. Hunter Burchell did not experience combat. His combat experience is simply unknown.

Growing up in rural Appalachia, Hunter was likely already familiar with guns when he enlisted. His Clay County home was not untouched by the feuds that kept Appalachian communities on edge during the late 1800s and early 1900s. The White-Howard feud in Clay County disrupted many innocent families, led to the state militia being deployed to Manchester to try to keep the peace, and eventually played a role in the assassination of Governor William Goebel in Frankfort in 1900. Finally, in 1901, "Articles of Peace" were drawn up and approved by representatives of each faction. One of those representing the Howard clan (which included the Garrard family) was Hunter Burchell's father, Dr. J.R. Burchell. Hunter was only seven years old at the time, but, as Hunter grew into a young man, the feud continued to erupt into skirmishes, including one battle that left two men dead and two wounded. Hunter was not unfamiliar with violence, and his childhood was immersed in arguments that were settled by gunfire. Hunter's term in the Army provided him with formal training in the use of firearms, a skill that may have served him well in France but landed him in significant trouble in Kentucky in January of 1932.

Other Burchell family members were not immune from the violent Clay County environment. Hunter's younger brother, John, along with two other men, was arrested for killing a sheriff and two deputies in September of 1921 when a gun battle erupted in the shower house of a coal camp in Lynch. In what appeared to be a labor dispute, the officers began shooting at John Burchell and his companions as they showered after a mining shift. John grabbed a pistol and returned fire, killing the three officers. John Burchell and his companions were acquitted at trial in 1922.

Upon returning home from the war, Hunter was a general laborer and lived with his mother in the family home. Dr. and Mrs. Burchell had divorced in 1921. Also, in 1921, Hunter married Ethel Sandlin in Manchester.

By 1930 Hunter was living and working as a farmer near Connors Station in Shelby County. All but subsistence farming suffered greatly during the Great Depression, and farming did not suit him. He soon was hired as a guard at the Kentucky State Reformatory in Frankfort. His brother, Jennings, was also a guard there, and his brother- in-law, William Roach, was the warden. The position of prison guard offered Hunter a steady government job with benefits. Hunter and Ethel moved in with Jennings in his bungalow on St. Clair Street in Frankfort.

In January of 1932, Warden Roach assigned Hunter to escort a prisoner, Floyd Miller, to Mt. Vernon, where he was to testify in the trial of his brother, Robert, who had been indicted for the same crime in which Floyd had been convicted, inappropriately accepting bank deposits after the People's Bank of Mt. Vernon had been declared insolvent. Those deposits had been funneled through the account of a friend, R.C. Haff, who was also prosecuted. Both brothers had both been accused, arrested, indicted, and one had been convicted for bank fraud.

This assignment should have been routine. In a normal situation, Hunter would have escorted the prisoner to Mt.

Vernon, where he would be lodged in the county jail at night and between court appearances. However, Hunter was allowing Miller to stay at his own home, and records indicate that Hunter was lodging there as well. Statements Hunter made later indicate that Warden Roach was aware of this arrangement and allowed it. Whether this was true is unknown. Hunter and Miller were seen about town, eating in restaurants, and generally enjoying Miller's furlough.

This did not sit well with the citizens of Mt. Vernon. Many had lost money when the People's Bank failed. They complained to Sheriff Tipton, who immediately called the Kentucky Attorney General, Bailey Wooten, who then contacted Warden Roach. Warden Roach apparently reprimanded Hunter. Hunter did not take it well.

On Saturday morning, January 16, 1932, Hunter stormed into the courtroom and loudly complained to Judge Roscoe Tarter, who was presiding over the Miller trial. Tarter asked Sheriff Tipton to escort Burchell from the courtroom. Noah and Burchell had an unpleasant confrontation in an adjacent room. No one witnessed that encounter.

At around six o'clock that evening, Sheriff Tipton was standing on Main Street, in front of the Cox Drug Store, talking with former Sheriff John Griffin, when Hunter Burchell approached him and shouted. Noah shoved him away. Burchell quickly drew his gun and shot Sheriff Tipton twice in the chest. Tipton fell and Burchell shot him twice more in the back of the head.

Hunter was quickly overpowered by Griffin and Deputy Carter, who had been standing nearby. Hunter was quickly transported to the Danville jail, thirty-five miles to the north, to avoid a mob lynching. Six weeks later he was transferred to Somerset, thirty-five miles west of Mt. Vernon, to stand trial. The Commonwealth had asked for the death penalty, and Hunter Burchell sat in jail, no doubt pondering his situation and worried about his fate.

Chapter Eight

NOAH'S GUN

America has had a love affair with guns since its beginnings. And, like most romances, it has been a love-hate relationship. From the time of the American Revolution through today's chaotic times, the one constant—both good and bad—has been the gun.

This country was wrenched from the British using guns. Guns were used to defeat the pro-slavery South, and finally cemented the states together into one United States. Guns defeated Nazi Germany and liberated concentration camps. But guns also facilitated controversial wars in Vietnam, Iraq, and Afghanistan.

Guns also played a critical role in America's westward expansion. Guns harvested game upon which hungry pioneers feasted. They allowed settlers to defend themselves against hungry predators, outlaws, and marauding Indians. But those same guns played a pivotal role in the extirpation of native wildlife and conquest of indigenous peoples.

Guns, to this day, play an incontrovertible role in our lives. We use them for recreation and hunting. We defend ourselves during home invasions, back-alley muggings, and convenience-store robberies. But those same guns are also used by home invaders, muggers, mass murderers, and terrorists. Americans own approximately three-hundred million firearms, an average of one gun per person. Like it or not, guns are a part of American culture.

Most firearms used for recreation, personal defense, and law enforcement are a product of war. With very few exceptions, just about every gun you see in gun stores, in home safes, and hanging over fireplaces had its origins in military settings. For example, the lever action Winchester and Marlin 30-30s our fathers and grandfathers used to harvest deer in the autumn woods can be traced back to the New Haven Arms Henry Rifle developed during the Civil War. Before the Henry, most rifles were breech loading rifles that had to be loaded one shell at a time. The Henry was manufactured for the Union Army and the southern troops called it the "damned Yankee rifle that they would load on Sunday and shoot all week."

After the war, Winchester took that design a bit further and created the 1866 "Yellow Boy", a lever action gun that used a brass-bronze alloy that gave it a distinctive golden sheen. Winchester further refined that gun and introduced a more reliable Model 1873 that became the "gun that won the west." Further changes and refinements evolved into the gun grandpa used to put venison on the Thanksgiving table. War had birthed a firearm that eventually became a cultural icon. And, as I was to discover, so it was with the gun carried by Sheriff Noah Tipton.

I always wondered about Noah's gun. What caliber was it? Who was the manufacturer? At one point in my research I discovered that one of my cousins, Dr. Preston Nunnelley, owns that gun. Preston and his wife, Lucille, had been very close to Lillie in her later years, and they inherited many of her belongings. My wife and I visited with Preston and Lucille, and over cake and coffee, I was able to examine Noah's gun.

I had two surprises. First, I was struck by how ordinary Noah's gun was. I'm not sure what I expected. Defense documents filed after Burchell's trial, attempting to justify the murder, indicated that Noah had a larger caliber weapon than Burchell, a ridiculous argument. However, if just the facts of the argument were true, then Noah must have been carrying a large caliber gun. So, I expected a 1911 semi-auto .45, a .45 caliber Smith revolver, or maybe even an old-style Colt .45 Peacemaker. But Noah's gun was a standard police-issue Smith and Wesson K Frame .38 special, a very unremarkable weapon.

The Smith and Wesson K-Frame .38 revolver was developed in 1899 as a reliable weapon for the military and later, law enforcement. It is often erroneously called the Model 10 (Smith didn't begin labeling guns with model numbers until 1957) and over six million were made, making it the most popular handgun of the twentieth century.

The second surprise was that Preston owns two of them. Apparently, after Noah's death and Lillie was appointed Sheriff (see Chapter 10), she acquired a handgun as well. I always assumed that Lillie carried Noah's gun. But, she didn't. She had her own. It is possible that during Burchell's arrest and the subsequent litigation, a process that took a half year, Noah's revolver may have been kept as evidence. It makes sense that Lillie would need a weapon, as she was appointed Sheriff within days of the murder. So, she obtained her own weapon.

Up until the early 1990s most rural law enforcement personnel, including those working for Rockcastle County, had to provide their own weapons. Where Noah and Lillie bought their revolvers is unknown. A fire that destroyed the Rockcastle County Courthouse took with it, among the files on Noah's murder, any records of firearm purchases. It is probable that the County purchased guns and was reimbursed out of officers' pay, but we'll never know for sure.

It is easy to imagine Noah's big calloused hands holding that gun. It fit his hand perfectly, and he held it like a ballplayer holds a familiar baseball, firmly and with purpose.

One of the Tipton guns had been in pretty bad shape... rusty, corroded, dirty...so it had been recently cleaned and re-blued, a process that collectors will tell you greatly diminishes the historical value of a gun. However, Sheriff Noah Tipton is not a widely recognized figure, so historical value was probably not a consideration.

So, what type of gun did Hunter Burchell use to kill Noah Tipton? If this murder had occurred today, the type of weapon Burchell used would be easily determined and recorded. The police report would probably describe the weapon. Noah's autopsy report would undoubtedly say something like "... the entry and exit wounds and recovered projectiles are consistent with the caliber of the weapon used by Burchell and the other unexpended rounds found in the weapon." Unfortunately, no police reports were preserved, and the autopsy report is long lost. The death certificate was signed by Dr. Monroe Pennington, a local family doctor who had delivered many of the sons and daughters of the citizens of Rockcastle County. The death certificate does indicate that an autopsy was completed, but the autopsy report has been lost or burned in the courthouse fire. Dr. Pennington did testify at Burchell's trial that Noah's gun was found at the undertaker's office underneath his coat and in a shoulder holster under his left arm. Pennington also testified that he examined the gun. In it were four live rounds and two expended shells. However, a further examination of the gun and the shells revealed that it had not been recently fired. Pennington smelled the gun and shells and checked the inside of the barrel for fresh gunpowder residue. He also testified that he found lint and dust in the barrel and under the hammer of the gun.

Quite often those who carry revolvers regularly leave the chamber under the barrel empty or holding an expended round to avoid a discharge if the weapon is dropped on its hammer. Why Noah had another expended round in the gun is unknown.

If Burchell was carrying a smaller caliber weapon, as was stated by his defense at trial, several possibilities come to mind. It is possible that Burchell was using a .22 rimfire revolver or a .22 semi-auto pistol. However, that is unlikely because the lightweight .22 projectile has very little "stopping power." A thick leather wallet, in a breast-pocket of a coat, for example, would dramatically decrease the penetration of the bullet.

Smith and Wesson and other manufacturers did make a .32 caliber revolver that Burchell may have carried. A more likely possibility is the Colt 1903 .32 auto "pocket pistol". This gun was sometimes used by military personnel because it has such a flat frame and sleek profile, making it more convenient to carry either in a leg holster, a shoulder holster, or in a coat pocket. This gun was also carried by gangsters and outlaws who wished to have a piece that could be easily concealed. Al Capone and John Dillinger both carried this pistol. Burchell would undoubtedly have come into contact with many such people as a prison guard. The fact that he was able to get off two very quick and accurate shots and another two after Noah fell, point to the Model 1903 as Burchell's gun.

A June 3, 1932 article in the *Interior Journal* newspaper in Stanford, Kentucky, reported that Hunter's gun was used as a court-ordered partial payment for stenographic services in preparing Hunter's appeal documents. The article reported that the bill for the services would be $600, but that the gun was only worth $15, around $450 in today's currency. The article described the firearm as a "pistol" rather than a gun or revolver. If the article's writer had a working knowledge of guns, he or she would know that the term "pistol" often refers to a semi-auto handgun, not a revolver, further reinforcing the theory that he used a Colt 1903 model .32 semi-auto pistol. The value of the gun also supports that premise. However, we have no knowledge of the writer's knowledge or expertise.

An interesting parallel emerged during my research on this topic. In 1924, the lawman Bill Tilghman was killed in Cromwell, Oklahoma. Bill Tilghman had been a well-known law enforcement figure in the late 1800s and around the turn of the century when he served with Wyatt Earp and as a deputy with Bat Masterson. He also made a name for himself as a no-nonsense lawman in Texas and Oklahoma and was best-known for capturing the outlaw Bill Doolin. Tilghman was hired out of retirement to clean up the town of Cromwell. He was seventy years old, but still had the reputation and demeanor to do the job. On the night of November 1st, he was attempting to disarm a seemingly-intoxicated Wiley Lynn, when Lynn's firearm discharged twice, inflicting fatal wounds. Bill Tilghman died twenty minutes later.

Several aspects of this case are similar to the murder of Noah Tipton. Noah and Bill Tilghman were both known as tough law officers. Of course, Noah's notoriety was local, but Tilghman's was national, due in part to his association with Earp, Masterson and his capture of Doolin. Both men were officers not to be taken lightly. Both Noah's and Tilghman's killers were also law officers. Burchell was a prison guard and Lynn was a Prohibition Agent. Both Burchell and Lynn were behaving erratically, and both may have been drinking. Additionally, both men fired more than one shot into their victims, a fact that could dispute an accidental discharge. Both Burchell and Lynn never paid for their crimes. Wiley Lynn was acquitted by a jury after tampering with witnesses, and Hunter Burchell's fate is discussed in Chapters 9 and 10.

Another parallel between the two killings worth mentioning is that the same type of firearm may have played a role in both. Tilghman had reportedly been recently diagnosed with cancer and carrying his heavy Colt Peacemaker .45 was painful. So, he had resorted to carrying a Colt 1903 auto "pocket pistol." In this instance, the man carrying the .32 was the one killed, but the parallels between the two incidents is still interesting.

Of course, the significance of the calibers of the guns supposes that Burchell's defense offered a grain of truth. Defense documents and the trial defense testimonies contain dozens of inaccuracies that were disputed by the prosecution witnesses and the records. Those documents and testimony are discussed further in Chapter 9. Those inaccuracies appear to be the result of a narrative fabricated by the defense to sway public opinion, the jury, and later, the appellate court. It is understandable that the team of Defense lawyers would go to great lengths to represent their client. However, fabricating a false narrative seemed to be an integral part of their legal strategy as well.

Four years before his own death, Noah was involved in an altercation that nearly cost him his life and may have affected the outcome of his confrontation with Hunter Burchell on the evening of January 16, 1932. Accompanied by Sheriff John Griffin and Railroad Special Agent Cam Mullins, the three men, acting on an anonymous tip, traveled to Mullins Station, a rural crossroads, to intercept a delivery of moonshine whiskey.

Mullins Station, an early pioneer settlement, is in a very remote area of Rockcastle County about five miles due east of Mt. Vernon. The presence of a railroad agent suggests that the whiskey was to be either off-loaded or smuggled onto a train at the freight depot that was there in 1932.

The three officers were attempting to arrest the four men with the whiskey when one of the perpetrators pulled a gun and, according to the *Stanford Interior Journal*, "the shooting got underway." Sheriff Griffin was shot in the chest and Noah was shot in the left hand and the head. Two of the bootleggers were killed in the gunfight. Lillie later said that Noah had shot and killed both men. This incident is discussed more fully in Chapter 6.

Noah's head wound was likely from a grazing shot, as there are no records or family memories of Noah having a serious

H. BURCHELL, PRISON GUARD, UNDER ARREST

Freedom Allowed Convicted Man Said To Have Led To Tragedy

4 BULLETS PIERCE BODY

N. J. Tipton, 55, Victim Of Fusilade Fired By Reformatory Guard

MT. VERNON, Ky., Jan. 16. (AP)— N. J. Tipton, 55, sheriff of Rockcastle county, was shot and killed tonight by Hunter Burchell, 30, guard at the state reformatory, whom the sheriff had accused of not properly guarding a convicted former bank cashier brought here to testify at the trial of his brother.

Burchell had brought Floyd E. Miller, former cashier of the People's bank here, under sentence of 13 years imprisonment, from the Frankfort reformatory Thursday to testify at the trial of his brother, R. H. Miller, assistant cashier.

Sheriff Tipton had called Bailey P. Wootton, state attorney-general at Frankfort and told him Burchell was allowing Miller to stay at his home instead of turning him over to the jailer. He said Burchell and his wife were visiting at the Miller home and the convicted man was being allowed to go about when and where he pleased.

Newspaper report on the arrest of Hunter Burchell.

Wathalyne Hendrick, the author's mother, at the Fallen Officer's Memorial at Eastern Kentucky University.

Coach Marvin Fairchild and his two daughters Geraldine and Wathalyne.

tion District No. ... 1 2 0

St., ... Ward)

d in a hospital or institution, give its NAME instead of street and number)

.... St., ... Ward. ....

(If nonresident, give city or town and State)

cs. ds. How long In U. S., if of foreign birth? yrs. mos. ds.

MEDICAL CERTIFICATE OF DEATH

16 DATE OF DEATH / 10 , 19 3 2

(Month) (Day) (Year)

17

I HEREBY CERTIFY, That I attended deceased

from *Jany 16*, 19 32 to *Jany 16*, 19 32,

that I last saw h _in_ alive on *after death*, 19 ,

and that death occurred on the date stated above at *7 0* m.

The CAUSE OF DEATH* was as follows: / 1 3

Gun Shot wound

- Violence -

.... (Duration) *Died Instantly* yrs. mos. ds.

Contributory ....

(Secondary)

.... (Duration) .... yrs. .... mos. .... ds.

18 WHERE WAS DISEASE CONTRACTED

if not at place of death? ....

Did an operation precede death? *No* Date of ....

Was there an autopsy? *Yes*

What test confirmed diagnosis? ....

(Signed) *M. Pennington*, M. D.

/ 20 , 19 3 2 (Address) *Mt Vernon*

*State the Disease Causing Death, or, in deaths from Violent
Causes, state (1) Means and nature of Injury; and (2) whether

Death Certificate of Noah Tipton

Retired Sheriff John Griffin

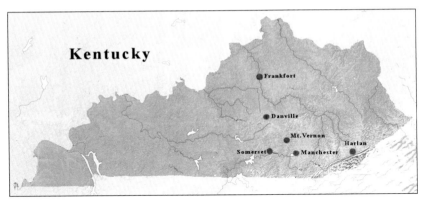

Map of Kentucky showing locations that played a role in this story.

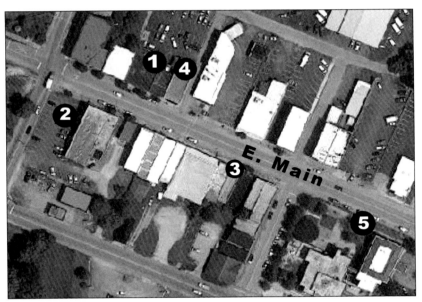

Downtown Mount Vernon featuring 1) Cox's Drug Store, 2) Miller Residence, 3) People's Bank, 4) Post Office, and 5) Courthouse.

The People's Bank Building

Cox's Drugstore

A Young Preston Nunnelley in Front of Cox's Drug Store, circa 1945

Sheriff Noah Tipton

Lillie Tipton

Lillie's Family, circa 1903. The photo was probably taken by Lillie.

Wathalyne as a teenager.

John Jack's grave in Harlan County.

Sarah Tipton, wife of John Jack.

Noah, Dolora, Lillie, and her sister Nancy, circa 1920.

Mt. Vernon Home of Noah and Lillie

Captured moonshine

Mullins Station Depot, the site of the 1927 Gunfight.

Cave near Mullins Station

Burchell family (Hunter at lower right), circa 1905

Burchell's Frankfort Home

Noah's and Lillie's Guns and Noah's Badge

Colt 1903 "Pocket Pistol", possibly the model used by Hunter Burchell.

Noah, with his coat buttoned, and his two granddaughters.

The Lindbergh headline

Judge Roscoe Tarter

Governor Ruby Laffoon

A Gift from Noah to Lillie.

Lillie's Iroquois Court Home

Lillie Tipton, circa 1965

Hunter Burchell (third from right), circa 1960

Noah Tipton's Funeral, with John Griffin in the center.

Wathalyne at the Tipton Gravesite

head wound. It must be noted that the last known photo of Noah clearly shows a diagonal scar above his left eye. It is possible that the scar was a result of that 1927 gunfight. Noah was right-handed, so day-to-day activities were probably unaffected by the wound to his left hand, even if the affects were longer-lasting. Family lore and the evidence suggests that when Hunter Burchell pulled a gun on Noah on that January evening four years later, Noah's buttoned overcoat prevented him from drawing his own weapon.

Out of curiosity, I tried an experiment. I strapped a holstered revolver to my right hip and buttoned up a long overcoat like the one worn by Noah. I attempted to quickly draw my weapon. I had to use my left hand to unfasten a button and pull the coat aside. I tried the same thing, only using a shoulder holster under my left arm. Again, I had to use my left hand to unbutton and pull back the coat. With a little practice, I was able do both maneuvers reasonably quickly. I tried the same thing, pretending that my left hand had been injured, by using only my right hand to perform the maneuvers. My speed decreased significantly. My conclusion was that even if Noah had enough time to retrieve his gun from under his coat, the four-year-old hand wound may have slowed him down. Of course, this is assuming he had enough time to even try to draw his gun. It is probable that Burchell already had his own weapon in his hand, in his pocket, planning to pull it at the least provocation. So, could that old injury have contributed to Noah's death?

This theory is pure speculation, but an interesting clue to reconstructing the events of that January evening.

On Easter Sunday morning, 1930, a photo was taken of Noah, my mother, and her sister. In the photo, Noah is wearing the overcoat he wore the day he was killed. Prophetically, the coat is buttoned. That photo is shown on the front cover of this book.

There is one line of reasoning that is decisive in determining whether or not Noah drew his weapon on Hunter Burchell during the altercation on January 16, 1932. If Noah Tipton had drawn and fired first, Hunter Burchell, *not* Noah Tipton, would have been lying dead in the street. When Noah shoved Burchell away, and Burchell drew his gun, Noah had no opportunity to draw his own weapon. Its caliber was completely irrelevant. Noah never had a chance.

Chapter Nine

The Trial

After a change in venue, William Hunter Burchell's trial for the murder of Noah Tipton was held from March 1 through March 7, 1932, in Somerset, Kentucky, a small town about twenty-five miles southwest of Mt. Vernon. Today, the drive from Mt. Vernon to Somerset takes about thirty minutes, but in 1932 it was closer to an hour and a half. Slower automobiles and poor roads separated the two communities, and a change in venue from Rockcastle County to Pulaski County ensured a pool of jurors with few preconceived notions and with few family or social connections to the victim or the accused. Despite one of Hunter Burchell's defense lawyers—J.C. Bird—strenuously objecting to the trial being held in Somerset and filing a second change in venue request, that objection met with no success.

In our modern legal environment, the time between an arrest and a trial in a homicide case can be several years. Our court systems are clogged and overwhelmed predominantly by drug-related crimes. Since 1932, our justice system has also become much more complicated by many more safeguards to protect the accused. Hunter Burchell was arrested on January 16 and his trial began on March 1. In 1932, justice was intended to be swift.

Another striking difference between trials in the 1930s and those of today is the manner in which trial transcripts are handled. In 1932, a trial stenographer would, in handwritten shorthand, record the events of the trial, the courtroom motions, testimonies, objections, and the words of the participants. Not until a verdict was reached and an appeal filed was the handwritten transcript typed. In this case, a verdict was reached and an appeal filed, but the transcript was never typed. The handwritten transcript of the Burchell Trial has been lost to time; however, the motions filed by the defense and the Commonwealth that were forwarded to the Court of Appeals do exist in the Kentucky State Archives. Those records, along with newspaper accounts of the trial and personal stories of those present are all we have available to piece together what occurred during the trial of Hunter Burchell.

In Kentucky, March is a month that straddles the line between the grays of winter and the greens of summer. The daffodils peek through the soggy carpet of winter leaves, but sometimes through an inch or two of crusty snow. March is also a month when Kentuckians never know how to dress. To a nine-year-old girl, comfortable woolens in the morning can become heavy and itchy in the afternoon as the promise of spring warms the air.

And so it was during the trial of Hunter Burchell. My mother, who was nine years old, remembered that the courtroom in Somerset was stifling hot. No doubt the coal furnace was fired up early, as the outside temperature was in the low forties. But by afternoon, the air had warmed to nearly seventy degrees outside, and the crowded courtroom was hot. Handkerchiefs were waving as lawyers and court officials were wiping their brows, and onlookers were creating tiny breezes with cardboard fans.

The jury selection took all day and the jury was pronounced complete the next morning, March 2. The jury was made up of twelve white men, ten of whom were farmers, one a bricklayer, and one a merchant.

Somerset's *Commonwealth* newspaper was a bi-weekly newspaper, a bit of a rarity for a small-town newspaper in the 1930s. During the week of Hunter Burchell's trial, the headlines were dominated by news of the courtroom goings-on. However, on March 2, 1932 that changed. The infant son of Charles and Anne Morrow Lindbergh had been kidnapped, an event that dominated the local and national headlines.

Charles Lindbergh was an American icon. In 1927 he became the first aviator to fly solo, non-stop, across the Atlantic Ocean, propelling him into a life of fame, prosperity, and eventual tragedy. His wealth and notoriety made him a target.

What would you do if you won the Powerball lottery? We have all had those thoughts.

Pay off your mortgage, set up a trust for your grandchildren, contribute to charity? One of the first items on your list should be setting up a security plan for your family. Being extraordinarily wealthy puts a bullseye on the backs of your family members. Kidnapping one of them, particularly one of the children, for ransom, would be a constant threat. And that is exactly what happened to little Charles Lindbergh, Jr.

On the night of March 1, 1932, the twenty-month old child was taken from his crib, carried through his bedroom window, down a ladder, and into American history as the victim of the crime of the century. His partially buried remains were discovered three months later by a truck driver who pulled to the side of a lonely road to relieve himself in the adjacent forest. Eventually, Bruno Richard Hauptmann was arrested, tried, and convicted of the crime.

Despite many conspiracy theories surrounding Hauptmann's arrest and conviction, the circumstantial and physical evidence pointing to his guilt were overwhelming.

Hauptmann had possessed and spent some of the marked ransom money. His handwriting and grammar matched the ransom note. Wood found in his attic was an identical match to the wood and saw marks on the ladder used to climb into the baby's window. His financial records showed large unaccounted-for deposits. And, his whereabouts matched the locations of the perpetrator of the crime and ransom exchanges. Whether or not he acted alone has never been determined, but he was clearly guilty.

No one to this day knows why little Charles Jr. was killed. An autopsy showed that he was killed by blunt-force trauma to the head. He could have been accidentally dropped as he was being carried down the ladder. He could have been purposely killed to silence his crying during the abduction. It is possible the killer planned the murder from the start to avoid extra baggage while fleeing the crime. No matter what the motive, Hauptmann sealed his own fate when he left the baby in the underbrush beside a lonely road. Hauptmann was executed on April 3, 1936.

The following excerpt is from The *Somerset Commonwealth* newspaper and describes the mood of the nation after the kidnapping:

"No crime in recent history has so aroused the entire American public as the kidnapping of the young son of Col. and Mrs. Charles A. Lindbergh. Little Charles Augustus Jr. is the nation's baby. He is a national character and has been since he was born. His abduction was a dastardly crime resented by every red-blooded American, children and grown-ups alike. Every parent grieved with the stricken father and mother. They knew the anguish they endured. They could feel the heart-throbs and immeasurable grief. They could realize what the finding of the empty crib meant to the grief-stricken parents. They knew the darkness that settled over Colonel and Mrs. Lindbergh as they viewed the dirty foot-tracks left by the villains, and the ladder on the lawn outside the window, that told so vividly the fate that had befallen their young son. It is one great

American heart that grieved with those grief-stricken parents."

The news of the Lindbergh kidnapping stole the Burchell trial headlines and was on the lips of all Americans on March 2nd, but the trial went on.

Knowing that he would be called to the stand as an eye-witness to the shooting of Noah Tipton, former Sheriff John Griffin sat on the front row of spectators. The last six weeks had been difficult for John. He had been standing only feet away from his best friend when Noah was gunned down. He had been a pallbearer at Noah's funeral, and had offered advice and encouragement to Noah's wife, Lillie, as she assumed the office of Rockcastle County Sheriff. Moreover, he had seen the various motions filed by Burchell's impressive team of defense attorneys. John felt like justice would be served, but he was uneasy.

(It must be noted that it is rare in today's trials for a witness to be in the courtroom observing the trial and testimonies of other witnesses. However, my mother clearly remembered John Griffin's presence during the trial. Perhaps in 1932, those rules and customs were different.)

John reflected on the events that led him to this front row seat in a courtroom in Somerset, Kentucky. A year earlier, Floyd Miller had been convicted of defrauding the Peoples Bank of Mount Vernon and sentenced to a three-year sentence at the Kentucky State Penitentiary in Frankfort. Floyd's brother, Robert Miller had also been charged with the same crime, and his trial was underway when Floyd was brought back to Mt. Vernon to testify in the trial.

John Griffin looked around the courtroom and glanced down at his hands. They were trembling. He was bursting with anger. These men had stolen his money and money earned by the hard-working citizens of Mt. Vernon. And look what it caused.

Floyd Miller had been guarded by Hunter Burchell, a corrections officer at the prison. Floyd was carousing with Hunter rather than spending his nights in the county jail. The angry citizens of Mt. Vernon complained to Sheriff Tipton and Noah, in turn, called Kentucky Attorney General, Bailey Wooten. Wooten called Warden William Roach, who reprimanded Burchell. That was when serious trouble started. Burchell stormed into the courtroom where Miller was being tried, and Judge Roscoe Tarter had Noah remove Burchell from the courtroom. They had a confrontation in the adjacent jury room, and Burchell stormed out, angry and humiliated. He then returned that evening and shot Noah down in the street.

John's mind drifted into a dark place. Could he have reacted faster, tackling Burchell *before*, not *after* Noah was shot? "Could I have saved him?"

John remembered trying to control the chaos that ensued. Burchell was overpowered and arrested on the spot and taken to the Danville jail the same night to prevent a lynching.

John wondered if he should have simply let the citizens of Mt. Vernon have their way and lynched this little man from a light pole. But he knew Noah wouldn't have wanted that kind of justice.

Noah's widow, daughter, and grandchildren needed support, so John had helped arrange Noah's funeral, and had served as a pallbearer.

Working with deputies Abney and Carter, he coordinated the business of the Sheriff's office until Lillie could set aside her grief and serve as the newly named Sheriff. And John assisted with the Commonwealth's case against Hunter Burchell.

John Griffin had preferred having the trial in Mt. Vernon, where the prosecution might have the home field advantage. However, the defense team filed a motion for a change in venue, fearing just such an advantage, and it was granted on January 19th. The defense motion for Burchell's bail and a motion to remove Circuit Judge Tarter from the case were both denied. On January 27th, Hunter Burchell was escorted from the Danville jail to supposedly be moved to the jail in Stanford. However, when he arrived in Stanford, the deputies guarding him opened sealed orders to take him on to Somerset. John knew about the sealed order, and he had recommended the clandestine trip from Stanford to Somerset for the prisoner's protection.

Circuit Judge Roscoe Tarter was also the presiding judge in Hunter Burchell's trial. The defense team had filed a motion to have Tarter recused from this trial; that motion had been denied by Tarter himself, a move that provided the defense one solid reason for an appeal. Tarter had been in the courtroom in Mt. Vernon the morning of the crime and had ordered Sheriff Tipton to remove Burchell after his outburst. Tarter was, therefore, a potential witness, and should not have presided over the trial. Additionally, Tarter and Sheriff Tipton were acquainted and had worked together in the past. It appears Judge Tarter's intent was to oversee the trial to ensure that justice was served. However, his presiding over the trial may have had the opposite effect.

John Griffin sat quietly throughout the jury selection on March 1st, and preliminary motions on March 2nd. On March 3rd, the Commonwealth's Attorney Sandusky summarized the case against Burchell with opening arguments.

The first witness for the prosecution was John Griffin. He testified that Burchell approached Noah at around 5:30 pm on January 16th and angrily shouted, "I hear you are telling that you rubbed your pistol in my face!" Noah then shoved Burchell away and said, "Go away! I don't want to argue on the street." Burchell drew his weapon and shot Noah twice in the chest. Noah fell and Burchell shot him twice more in the back of the head. John also testified that Deputy Carter was the first to tackle Burchell and that Carter's gun discharged into the air during the scuffle. Fifteen subsequent prosecution witnesses corroborated John's version of what happened.

The discharging of Carter's gun may have played a role in the confusion as to the number of shots fired.

On March 5th, the Commonwealth closed its case. Court was adjourned until the next day. On March 6th, the defense called L.V. Murrell, who claimed to be an eyewitness as well. Murrell testified that Noah drew his gun and fired first. This testimony shocked the courtroom. With that sudden revelation, true or not, the defense team had offered a glimpse of their strategy.

Not much is known about Murrell. Based on the testimony of other witnesses, it seems that Murrell's version was not true. He could have heard Carter's gunshot and seeing a scuffle in the waning light of that January evening, simply been confused. He could have had a grudge against Tipton from a previous conflict. Or he could have been paid for his perjury by Burchell's supporters. In one of her letters to Governor Laffoon after the trial, Lillie refers to an indictment for perjury against Murrell and another man. No record of those indictments exists today, and the Commonwealth Attorney may have simply not pursued the prosecution (see Lillie's letters in Chapter 10).

So, was Murrell lying, or did he just remember the events differently than the other witnesses? Memory is the faculty in the brain that allows information to be stored and retrieved. Generally, the hippocampus and the amygdala are the parts of the brain responsible for memory. Memory is a fluid concept. Memories of particular events held by those who tell the story can change over time. If one narrates a version of the story that is not accurate over a period of time, eventually, in the mind of the storyteller, that version becomes true. It is a new reality. That is one of the reasons that legends and myths are born and grow.

The story of Noah and Lillie told by my family was not particularly accurate. The man who first told me the family story back in the 1980s said that Noah had been killed by a "hit-man." My cousin, Preston, who owns Noah's gun, told me he thought Noah was killed by the prisoner, not the guard. Kenneth Hopkins story of Lillie's "gunfight" can neither be confirmed or denied because the historic records have been lost (see Chapter 10).

Often, those evolved stories account for gaps in logic. It may be more logical to believe that Noah's killer was a paid assassin rather than a man who was angry. Maybe it is soothing for a family to believe that it took a complex scheme to kill an important man, not that an angry little man with a gun could simply walk up to their beloved Noah and shoot him dead.

Murrell may have been lying, but, it was a dark evening. The lighting was poor. Murrell heard five shots. He saw a scuffle, and maybe his mind played tricks on his memory.

Next to testify was Hunter Burchell, who claimed that Sheriff Tipton had threatened him at gunpoint that morning and had drawn his gun and fired first that evening. It was clear that the defense was building a case, not for capital murder, but for self-defense.

One newspaper reported that Burchell also testified that on the evening of the killing that he had been inside of Cox's Drug Store and met Noah as he was leaving the building. This testimony was clearly designed to insinuate that his encounter with Noah was mere happenstance and that he was not seeking out Noah, looking for a fight. a notion that could undermine the prosecution's stance that Burchell approached Noah with premeditation to do him harm. It appears that Hunter Burchell was the only witness who offered this version of the story. All of others said Burchell approached Noah from the sidewalk outside of the store.

Had Noah fired first and Hunter simply returned fire four times, totaling five shots? Or had Hunter shot first, hitting Noah four times, and had the fifth shot been from Deputy Carter's gun? The existing record shows that two witnesses claimed Noah shot first (one was immediately impeached on cross-examination). The other sixteen witnesses claimed Noah never even drew his weapon. Murrell's testimony provided a glimmer of doubt. As was surmised in Chapter 7 of this book, had Noah shot first, Burchell, not Noah Tipton would have been killed.

The motive for this murder has been a mystery that has troubled me. Beginning with the first time I heard the story back in 1982, the motive had been the driving force behind my research. Was Burchell simply angry at Noah? Was he a paid assassin? These questions were on my mind when I decided to drive to Clay County for answers. I drove down I-75 from Lexington to London, turned east on the Hal Rogers Parkway, and got off the Parkway at the Manchester exit. My first impression of Manchester, the county seat of Clay County, was what I expected. Fast food and gas stations greeted me. I continued into town and found a quaint central business district, not unlike Mt. Vernon's.

I spent some time that afternoon talking with a helpful lady at the local newspaper about Hunter and his family. She shared a book published by the county historical society that had a couple of references to Hunter...how he had been a construction contractor and had mentored his nephew, also named Hunter.

The newspaper's archives were housed in the public library, so I looked through the library's collection of microfilm. Unfortunately, the newspapers from the years surrounding the murder had been lost in a fire at the newspaper office.

I stopped by a local funeral home and was directed to the Burchell Family Cemetery, in the woods behind the newer

Memorial Gardens. I found the cemetery and parked my car at the gate. It was unlocked, so I went in and walked from headstone to headstone, looking for Hunter. On the second pass I found a strong possibility…William H. Burchell, born 1894, died 1972. The Lexington newspaper article published the day after the killing listed Burchell as being thirty years old. Could the paper have been eight years off?

I drove back into the little downtown and walked back into the library. I found the obituary of a William Hunter Burchell 1894-1972. Surely there would not have been two Hunter Burchell's in the same generation. He had, according to the obit, been a church-going, productive citizen.

This was a new twist in my journey. I had envisioned Hunter as an evil little rat-of-a- man, a coward who had shot down my beloved Noah in cold blood. How could the Hunter Burchell that I had found be the same person?

I was pretty sure of several facts and deductions. First, Hunter had not been carrying out the intent of his job as a prison guard by allowing Floyd Miller free run of the town. Secondly, he lashed out at Noah, the sheriff, a man in a position of authority who was simply doing his job. Thirdly, he approached Noah in a confrontational manner, drawing his pistol. All of these are facts and the deductions paint a pretty dark picture.

So, objectively, why did Hunter Burchell kill Noah Tipton?

My son, Dan Carman, is a successful criminal defense lawyer and former U.S. Marine Corp JAG. When it comes to violent crimes and motives for their commission, Dan has seen it all. Dan and I spent an afternoon reviewing documents pertinent to this case, and particularly the motive behind the murder.

Homicide, or the killing of one person by another, is usually committed for one or more of the following reasons:
- Accidental death, such as an automobile accident
- Acts of war

- Revenge
- Anger
- Impairment by drugs or alcohol
- Profit or greed
- Mental illness
- Love or a love triangle
- Pride
- Institutional justice, such as executions
- Defending another person or family member
- Defending one's honor
- Self defense

In this case, it is safe to rule out accidental death, acts of war, a love triangle, and defending another person. The motive of revenge would be a stretch and there is no evidence to suggest that Noah harmed anyone that Burchell knew. This murder was obviously not a case of institutional justice.

There is also no evidence to suggest that Hunter Burchell had any mental impairment

It is possible that he had post-traumatic stress disorder from his military service in World War I, but he was a mess sergeant, and may have seen minimal combat. There is no record of him being treated for "shell shock," an early euphemism for PTSD.

It is possible that Hunter had been drinking prior to the murder. This argument is strengthened by the fact that he stormed into the courthouse and publicly lashed out at Noah, a man who was in a position of authority simply doing his job. Why would a sober man do that? There were no witnesses to the confrontation that occurred after Judge Tarter had Noah remove Burchell from the courtroom, but that confrontation was obviously very unpleasant. Burchell left the courthouse and theoretically had all afternoon to drink and further fuel his anger. Inebriation is no excuse for murder, but alcohol does often bring out the darkness in otherwise good men. The reasonably good qualities he exhibited later in his life could have been the result of a subsequent life of sobriety. I reached out to Jean Burchell again, and she replied to me in a letter that her research indicated that Hunter and his brothers no doubt drank socially, but there is no family lore suggesting he was an alcoholic.

The profit motive is an interesting theory. When I first heard about Noah's death, back in 1981, I was told that he had been killed by a "hit man", suggesting that someone paid Burchell to kill Noah. If Burchell had been a professional assassin, he wasn't a very good one. He committed this crime in public in front of witnesses. It is possible, however, that the Miller brothers had paid him to kill Noah. Noah was a witness in the Miller trial, and his testimony could have been damaging. If this is the case, it is probable that any financial "arrangement" would have been a poorly thought out spontaneous deal offered by the Millers the afternoon of the crime. There is no available evidence to suggest that this occurred.

Anger and pride are certainly possibilities. Noah Tipton was a big, strapping man, a product of farming and physical labor. He was well over six feet tall. Hunter Burchell was a small man. His Army records indicate that he was five foot eight, but a family photo of him surrounded by other family members clearly shows that he was much smaller. Much like high school football teams tend to exaggerate the sizes of the players on rosters, the size of many Army inductees was sometimes exaggerated, especially if they were young. Based on photographs, it appears as though he was five foot six or smaller. It is possible that Hunter had what is commonly called the "little man" complex, or the "Napoleon complex." Smaller men sometimes tend to overcompensate for their size, especially if they are insecure. This overcompensation often results in a short temper and an easily bruised ego. According to Jean Burchell, her husband Bob remembered his father, Jennings Burchell, telling him, "Don't make Hunter mad!" The confrontation in the courthouse could have been the trigger that angered Hunter, and that anger simmered all day, resulting in him shooting Noah that evening.

There is some evidence to suggest that the Miller brothers had animosity toward Noah Tipton. After they were arrested for bank fraud, they had to liquidate some of their assets in Mt. Vernon to reimburse the embezzled funds and pay legal fees. Several of their properties were publicly auctioned, and Noah Tipton purchased two of those properties. This had to rankle the Millers, and no doubt helped fuel the simmering anger in Burchell as he spent the afternoon before the murder stewing at the Miller home.

There is also one newspaper refence to the fact that Warden Roach, Hunter's brother-in- law, had been upset with Tipton when Floyd Miller arrived at the State Prison to begin his sentence because he was not properly escorted and did not have the proper paperwork. That could have led to Roach directing Burchell to allow Miller to run free as a "slap" to Noah's face. Miller's improper arrival in Frankfort could have been an intentional slight, but it is doubtful, because there is no record that Tipton had any previous contact with Roach. It was probably just an oversight, or the whole conflict may have been a newspaper exaggeration. There is no evidence that Noah Tipton and Hunter Burchell had ever met prior to the Miller trial in January of 1932.

All of these motives suggest varying degrees of premeditation and could result in the charges of capital murder. The motives that could reduce a potential capital murder conviction to a manslaughter conviction would be self-defense and spontaneous anger. And that is exactly what Hunter's defense attorneys focused on.

The Defense summarized its case and on March 7th, Judge Tarter presented his instructions to the jury. They are as follows and are paraphrased here for clarity:

1. The jury shall consider the words "willful" as intentional, "feloniously" as committed with deliberate evil intentions, and "with malice aforethought" as predetermination to commit the act.
2. If the jury believes that Hunter Burchell, beyond a reasonable doubt, willfully, feloniously, and with malice aforethought killed Noah Tipton, the jury shall find Hunter Burchell guilty as charged and fix a punishment of either death or life in prison.
3. If the jury believes that Hunter Burchell, beyond a reasonable doubt, killed Noah Tipton without malice aforethought, and in the heat of passion, the jury shall find the defendant guilty of voluntary manslaughter and fix a penalty of not less than two years or more than twenty years in prison.
4. The jury shall find the defendant guilty of voluntary manslaughter if they believe Burchell did kill Tipton, but they have a reasonable doubt as to the motive. The penalty Tarter advised was between two and twenty years in prison.
5. If the jury believes, beyond a reasonable doubt, that Burchell acted in defense of his own life, the jury shall find him not guilty.
6. If the jury believes that Burchell initiated the conflict that led to Tipton's death, the jury can *not* find Burchell not guilty.
7. If the jury has reasonable doubt of the defendant having been proven guilty, then the jury shall find him not guilty.

When Judge Tarter dismissed the jury to a room adjacent to the courtroom to render the verdict John Griffin was overcome with a sense of dread. The defense team had done a good job at painting Noah's death, not as a cold-blooded murder, but as a disagreement that had escalated into a violent argument. John hoped for justice but was deeply concerned that justice would not be the result of this trial.

Onlookers from both the Burchell and Tipton factions broke into small groups in the courthouse hallways to quietly discuss the trial. A few left the courthouse to walk down the street for sandwiches and coffee. My mother and her sister sat on a bench at the rear of the courtroom, attempting to be quiet but occasionally poking and prodding each other as children will do.

The jury was out for just two hours, from 7:40 p.m. until 9:40 p.m. The jury filed back into the courtroom and announced a verdict of manslaughter and recommended a two year prison sentence.

After the verdict was read by the jury and Judge Tarter sentenced Hunter Burchell to two years of incarceration, the courtroom was nearly silent. Members of both factions, neutral onlookers, and the press sat, stunned. No one was happy with the verdict or the sentence. Burchell supporters had hoped for a not-guilty verdict. Tipton supporters hoped for either the death sentence or at least a long prison term.

It must be noted that many newspapers carried the news of this trial. Perhaps the most complete coverage was in Somerset's *Commonwealth* newspaper, which had a reporter in the courtroom throughout the trial. In reading all the newspaper coverage, including that of the Commonwealth, I found no record of Hunter Burchell saying anything when he was sentenced. Many judges will allow the defendant to speak, to have an opportunity to apologize to the family of those harmed, to express remorse. We do not know if Judge Tarter gave Burchell that opportunity. If he did, Hunter either declined to speak, or what he said was not newsworthy.

John Griffin remained in his seat after spectators began filing out. He glanced over at Lillie and choked back a sob. How could the justice system have failed this good woman. His mind again drifted into dark territory, a place where he contemplated that he could have saved Noah. He had seen the reflection of Burchell's gun in Noah's eyes. Could he have acted faster?

John shook his head violently, gagging on that question. "Don't go there," he whispered to himself.

John got up from the wooden chair in the front row of the Pulaski County Courthouse, smoothed his coat, and straightened his tie. Turning to leave, he placed his hand on Lillie's shoulder. He couldn't look at her, but he gently squeezed it. Then he walked out of the courtroom into the March air.

The result of this trial was like a stab to the heart for Lillie Tipton. As the courtroom began to empty, onlookers left, shaking their heads, whispering. Lillie sat in her chair until the room was empty. John's small gesture had been heartening, but barely. Tears of grief and anger streamed down her face. She knew that Hunter Burchell would spend the next two years in the State Prison, a ward of the warden who was his brother-in-law, probably guarded by his brother, and visited every day by his wife, who lived just a few blocks away. Two years, just two years. But the worst was yet to come.

I have always believed that Hunter Burchell approached Noah Tipton that rainy evening with his hand on his gun in his pocket. I believe that Hunter hoped Noah would draw his own weapon, but his plan went awry when Noah's buttoned coat prevented that from happening. I believe he approached Noah with the express intent to kill him, and the murder was premeditated. Hunter's anger simmered and finally boiled over that evening. However, Noah was my family, and perhaps my opinion is clouded by familial ties. The jury, after hearing all the testimony, believed that the appropriate verdict was manslaughter. However, the penalty of just two years in prison, in my opinion, does not fit the evidence. Burchell could have received up to twenty years confinement. Ironically, the fact that Judge Tarter did not recuse himself was probably grounds for an appeal that may have resulted in a new trial, and eventually Hunter Burchell may have gone free.

The Commonwealth Attorney could also have appealed the decision but did not. The defense team had cast that shadow of reasonable doubt necessary to save Hunter Burchell's life.

I have often wondered if there was anything that Sheriff Noah Tipton could have done differently that may have changed the tragic ending to this story. I have concluded that simply leaving his coat unbuttoned the evening of January 16 may have changed the course of events, but whether or not to button one's coat is not a decision that normally has life and death consequences. How could he have known? But maybe, had the confrontation earlier that morning been different, the outcome could have saved Noah's life.

I reached out to Tom Pyzic, a retired Lt. Colonel and Army Ranger with extensive combat experience, who is also a retired Kentucky State Police Lt. Colonel, Special Response Team member and training instructor. I asked Tom what Noah could have done differently. After telling Tom the story and outlining the sequence of events on January 16, Tom told me that Sheriff Tipton exhibited "great restraint" that morning during the confrontation at the courthouse. Tom suggested that Tipton could have arrested Burchell on the spot and charged him with either disorderly conduct or menacing, or the equivalent charge in the 1930s. Either charge, while slight, would have lodged Burchell in the County Jail to cool off.

Hunter testified at trial that Noah pulled a gun on him at the courthouse that morning. Based on his experience, Tom told me that if an officer pulls a gun on someone, usually that person is either shot or arrested.

Because the courthouse altercation occurred on a Saturday morning, had Hunter Burchell been arrested, he probably would not have been released from the county jail until Monday at the earliest. He would have had little if any contact with the Miller brothers to encourage his anger on Saturday or Sunday, and the whole episode may have been resolved on Monday, particularly if Warden Roach had intervened and brought Hunter back to Frankfort.

However, looking back on the events of January 16, 1932 with a critical eye toward learning law enforcement lessons is only an academic exercise. On that fateful January evening, the dark stars lined up. A winter's rain caused Noah to button his overcoat. A basketball game brought him to the Main Street sidewalk. A post office visit brought my mother to within earshot. A simmering disagreement over how to guard a prisoner reached the boiling point in a man, who all his life had been temperamental because of his size and violent environment. And that man had a gun.

As Hunter Burchell sat in the Danville jail throughout January and February awaiting trial he was interviewed by the local newspaper. He was reportedly pacing in his cell and acting like "he hadn't a worry in the world." Perhaps he was confident in his defense team and defense strategy. But he may have known that "the fix was in."

Hunter Burchell had received a shamefully light sentence, but his defense team was not finished. They filed an immediate appeal to the Kentucky Court of Appeals.

Chapter Ten

AFTERMATH

Hunter Burchell's appeal was filed by his defense lawyers immediately after the verdict recommending two years in prison was reached. Throughout the months of March and April, Hunter Burchell's defense team gathered and filed the materials needed for the appeal, including a motion to have Hunter declared a "pauper." This move would allow the Commonwealth to pay for the trial transcript preparation, a significant investment in those days. Burchell even offered to give the court transcriptionist his gun in exchange for typing the court records (see Chapter 7, "Noah's Gun"). It appears as though Hunter's family, who had no doubt paid for his defense team, may have been running out of patience with the normal procedures a defendant uses to avoid prison. This motion was denied.

During this period, Lillie received word that Hunter's family had approached Kentucky's governor, Ruby Laffoon, requesting a pardon for Hunter. Lillie was still reeling from the loss of her husband and the trial, but she would not let justice be denied without her own fight.

Governor Ruby Laffoon was born in a log cabin near Madisonville, Kentucky, on January 15, 1869. He was known as the "Terrible Turk from Madisonville," and served as Governor of the Commonwealth of Kentucky on the Democratic ticket, from 1931 through 1935. His administration was famous for political infighting, even among Democrats. Laffoon had little support, even from his Lt. Governor, A.B. "Happy" Chandler. At one point during his administration, Laffoon was in Washington meeting with President Franklin Roosevelt. Because he was out of state, the office of Governor, by law, was assumed by Lt. Governor Chandler. While Laffoon was away, Chandler called a quick session of the state legislature, and passed a bill that Laffoon had fought, instituting a state primary election system. The bill was signed into law, a huge defeat for Laffoon. During Laffoon's four years as Governor, he was able to enact the first Kentucky sales tax, a move that no doubt led to his unpopularity. He is perhaps best- known for instituting the ceremonial Order of Kentucky Colonels, and one of his first appointments was to a restauranteur, Harlan Sanders, who became known nationwide as Colonel Sanders. Late in his term as Governor, Laffoon retreated to an "insane asylum" to be treated for exhaustion. Laffoon died in 1941. Chandler went on to serve as Governor and eventually Commissioner of Major League Baseball. In that capacity, he facilitated the signing of Jackie Robinson, the first African American in Major League Baseball.

When Lillie received word of a potential pardon for Hunter Burchell, she wrote the governor a letter, knowing that the Burchell family was playing their political cards. Lillie was a tough woman, and decided to play that game as well.

First, she sat down in the rocking chair in her small living room and scribbled what she wanted to say, how she felt. When she read it over she knew it was disorganized and confusing. She rewrote it and it sounded much better. She folded the letter and placed it in Noah's Bible. The next day she carried the Bible to the Sheriff's office. She smoothed the pages and typed the letter. She then called John Griffin. When he arrived, she handed him the neatly typed pages. He sat down and read them slowly.

John looked up from the pages and into her eyes and said, "Lillie, Noah would be proud."

Lillie sent the letter to Governor Laffoon, and a carbon-copy to the *Louisville Courier Journal*, the largest newspaper in Kentucky.

For the first time in months, Lillie felt relieved. She had little expectation of a positive result, but she was actually doing something, rather than sitting back and allowing the monstrous weight of the judicial system crush her.

As word reached Lillie that the Governor was actually considering the pardon, she repeated the process. When she was told that the Governor had granted the pardon, she wrote another letter to him and again sent a copy to the newspaper.

Those letters are found at the end of this chapter. The first two letters requested that Governor Laffoon hold a hearing before considering Burchell's pardon. Laffoon's secretary, H.H. Holman, replied, stating that should Laffoon consider a pardon, a hearing would be held. It was not.

Rockcastle County, Kentucky, was a heavily Republican county. Noah Tipton was elected Sheriff on the Republican ticket. Clay County, the home of Hunter Burchell, was heavily Democrat. Hunter's family was affluent, and his father was a prominent local physician. It is certainly possible that the Burchell family reached out to the Democrat political machine surrounding Governor Ruby Laffoon to request a pardon, concerned about their son's safety in a prison where he may be surrounded by prisoners who bore the brunt of Hunter's temper.

Purchasing pardons is not unusual in dirty politics. While somewhat rarer in today's watchdog climate, currying political gain and campaign contributions by issuing pardons to felons was a well-used weapon in the arsenal of Ruby Laffoon. He pardoned nearly six-hundred felons before he left office, more than any other Kentucky Governor, before or since.

This quote, from Harry Caudill's 1963 book, *Night Comes to the Cumberlands*, might be an appropriate comment on Burchell's pardon:

"Lives were taken in defense of life, home or property, but most occurred in what Kentucky law terms 'sudden heat of passion.' Such cases arise in 'sudden affray,' when the killer is aroused by such a provocation on the part of the person slain as 'is reasonably calculated to arouse the passions of an ordinarily prudent person beyond his control.' When such a killing occurs, Kentucky law permits the jury to reduce the homicide from murder to manslaughter and to impose a relatively lenient prison sentence. This is precisely what occurred in most cases. The *Hazard Herald* in its May 8, 1925 issue reported that five men had been tried for murder in the county's Circuit Court, and that in all the sentences together a total of only twenty-two years' imprisonment was meted out! To the jurors, human life was cheap, even as it was to the defendants whose cases they heard. One issue of the *Hazard Herald* reported that a thief was given two years for stealing a turkey, while at the same term of court another man was sentenced to two years in the State Reformatory for killing his neighbor. Nor were the governors who augustly presided over the affairs of the state any more strongly inclined to law enforcement. They made lavish use of the pardon power and commuted or voided sentences of hundreds of prisoners. Pardons were extended on the slimmest pretexts, without any kind of post-parole supervision, and without systematic effort to grant clemency to persons with a demonstrated capacity for rehabilitation. Most pardons were inspired by political considerations. If a convict had a numerous clan of politically active persons, His Excellency was likely to hear his pardon plea with compassion, but if a prisoner was friendless, his prospects were bleak."

Governor Ruby Laffoon's Executive Order, dated May 9, 1932, pardoning Hunter Burchell, listed several reasons why the pardon was issued. Those reasons are almost entirely based on inaccuracies and paint a false narrative of the killing. Those inaccuracies include:

- Judge Tarter hurried the jury to reach a verdict. Tarter may have mentioned the term of the Circuit Court in passing, but he denied hurrying the jury.
- Noah Tipton had a larger gun than Burchell's. While possibly true, it is irrelevant. The lethality of Burchell's weapon was demonstrated by the outcome.
- Noah drew his weapon and shot first. Sixteen eyewitnesses disputed that assertion.
- Noah was a "fractious" and "high tempered." There is no evidence to support this. He was a "no-nonsense" officer, but his constituents appreciated that.
- Noah had killed other men. While this is true, he was simply doing his job.
- Burchell was "law-abiding and even tempered". His actions on 1/16/32 dispute that.
- Laffoon received letters and petitions supporting Burchell. He does not mention the letters and petitions supporting Tipton and requesting a hearing on the matter.

Lillie's heartfelt letters fell on deaf ears and were in vain. The hearing, promised by the Governor, was never held. While Lillie's letters may have impacted Laffoon's standing amongst Kentucky voters who read them in the newspaper, they didn't prevent the Governor from issuing an Executive Order on May 9th, pardoning Hunter Burchell. Lillie wrote her third letter, rebuking Laffoon. Including the time spent in the Danville jail before the trial, Hunter Burchell served less than four months behind bars for murdering Sheriff Noah Tipton.

This line is from the letter than Lillie wrote to Governor Laffoon, who was, at the time, considering a pardon for Hunter Burchell:

> "I want you to come, in person or in mind, and with my daughter, two small granddaughters and myself, stand by the mound in the back row of graves in our cemetery, where a grave, not sixty days old, holds the dearest part of my life: my protector from cold and hunger, my support in sickness, in health, my companion at home and at church, my defender during the troubles of life, who ruthlessly, wantonly, and with malice taken from me."

Lillie Tipton's letters to Governor Ruby Laffoon are a sad testament to the devastation that can be brought on by the misuse of political power. Those letters are included, in their entirety, at the end of this chapter.

Just three weeks before his murder, Noah had presented Lillie with a Christmas gift that she always cherished, a crystal jar with a sterling silver lid engraved with her initials, LT. Until her own death, she kept it on her bedroom dressing table, a reminder of her husband's love. Over the years, as she sat quietly at the table, brushing her hair, or freshening her lipstick, sometimes she saw a flickering shadow in the crystal prism. She wondered if it was Noah, standing behind her, offering his protective strength. It gave her hope. Her daughter, Dolora, inherited it, and left it to my mother. It now sits on an end table in our bedroom, a daily reminder of their love, where my wife and I can enjoy its beauty.

In 1935, Lillie Tipton sued Hunter Burchell for $50,000 in damages for killing her husband. The two-day trial was held in Stanford, Kentucky, after the defendant, Burchell, was awarded a change in venue. The defendant was represented by former Judge Manning and F.P. Stivers of Manchester. The plaintiff's attorneys were former Judge Sam Lewis of Mount Vernon, and Roscoe Tarter, who was the same judge who presided over Burchell's criminal trial. On November 26, 1935, Lillie was awarded $3,500, a tidy nest egg, but not nearly enough to compensate her for the loss of her beloved husband.

On Wednesday, January 20, 1932, four days after Noah's death, the Rockcastle County Fiscal Court voted to appoint Lillie Tipton as Sheriff. The Fiscal Court, called the County Court back in 1932, was made up of fifteen members, and the vote was unanimous. In addition to Lillie's appointment, Deputies Carter and Abney were re-appointed, as was Richard Anglin and J.J. Saylor. Anglin was currently serving as Jailer. One newspaper reported that Lillie was bedridden with grief and she did not immediately did not accept the appointment. However, she soon became Sheriff Lillie Tipton.

In the 1930s, female sheriffs in Kentucky were very rare. In those early days, most were appointed after the death of their husbands who had been sheriff. The process was known as "widow's succession" Two early women who gained notoriety in the field were Pearl Carter Pace and Florence Riney.

Pearl Pace, who was one of the first females actually elected to the position, was the Sheriff of Cumberland County from 1937 through 1942. She was a very "hands-on" officer and was known as "Pistol Packin' Pearl."

Florence Riney succeeded her husband as Davies County Sheriff after his death in 1936. She gained national media attention when she presided over the hanging of Rainey Bethea, a black man who had been convicted of raping a white woman.

According to an interview I conducted with Kenneth Hopkins, Lillie's nephew, at a Helton family reunion in 2016, many viewed Lillie's appointment as honorary, a way for the grieving widow to receive some compensation for Noah's death by receiving a county salary. Lillie, however, took the job very seriously. Records indicate that she made arrests, served warrants, and supervised the comings and goings of her deputies. Kenneth remembered her wearing a revolver in a holster around the waist of her skirt.

One incident described by Kenneth Hopkins is worth reporting. It seems as though Lillie and Deputy Abney had tracked a man who had murdered his whole family to a cabin in the mountains. They made a plan to simultaneously burst into the cabin from the front and rear doors and arrest the man. However, their timing was off, and before Abney could rush the cabin, he heard Lillie shout, followed by a gunshot. When Abney did burst through the door, Lillie was standing over a lifeless body. The dead man was holding a gun. Lillie claimed that the man committed suicide. But Abney always suspected that Lillie had killed the murderer. In the days before CSI, forensics, and crime scene protocol, Lillie's story was taken at face value.

This incident can neither be confirmed nor documented. Courthouse records were lost or destroyed, and coincidentally, all of the regional small-town newspapers from late January until the end of 1932 have also been lost. It is a great story, and there is no doubt that this incident, or at least some version of it, did occur, but the details have been lost to time.

My mother spoke sadly of a letter that Lillie received in the 1950s from Hunter Burchell. In it, Hunter asked for forgiveness. Lillie did not respond to the letter, choosing to destroy it instead. Mom, a strong Christian, believed in the power of forgiveness, but for Lillie, the murder of her husband was unforgiveable. In those days, people burned their trash. Lillie crumpled the letter and burned it in the backyard trash pit with the other worthless debris she had collected.

Lillie Tipton's 1935 lawsuit against Hunter Burchell achieved a degree of closure for her. The years of violence, beginning in 1927 when Noah survived the Mullins Station gunfight, were over. And so went the years of fear experienced by America as a whole. Prohibition was repealed in 1933. Al Capone was living his life as an inmate at Alcatraz. George Machine Gun Kelly was also spending his life in prison. Bonnie Parker and Clyde Barrow had been killed on a lonely road in Louisiana, and John Dillinger had been shot down as he left a movie theater in Chicago. President Franklin Roosevelt has told the country that "The only thing we have to fear is fear itself." Americans overcame those fears, braved the Great Depression, and had emerged stronger for it. So did Lillie Tipton.

Lillie's earnings from the lawsuit were used to invest in the modest real estate market in Mt. Vernon. She purchased several small frame houses from which she realized a steady rental income.

The Second World War impacted Mt. Vernon like it did in every small town in America. People purchased War Bonds, rationed goods, and young men went to war. Lillie's family was not exempt from service. Bentley Mullins, the man who would marry Lillie's widowed daughter, Dolora, served in the Army Engineer Corps. Lillie's granddaughter, Geraldine, had married and her young husband, Preston Nunnelley, Sr. served in the Marine Corps in the South Pacific. My mother's boyfriend, a pilot in the Army Air Corps, was killed in a training accident. And my father, who met and married Mom after the war, served in the Navy. Lillie, like many women during that period, maintained the home front, helping with the grandchildren, tending to her rental properties, and listening to the evening radio for news of the War.

John Griffin, who played a primary role in this tragedy, was also greatly affected by Noah's death and its aftermath. On August 2, 1932, just six months after Noah's murder, John suffered a stroke and died. He was sixty-two years old. He is buried at the Elmwood Cemetery, not far from his friends, Noah and Lillie.

By the time I was born and knew Lillie two decades later, she had bought two modest homes on Iroquois Court in Lexington. For many years she lived in one and the other was occupied by various family members, including her great grandson, Preston Nunnelley, and his wife, Lucille. Preston was in medical school at the University of Kentucky, and they took care of Lillie in her last years.

My memories of Lillie's Iroquois Court home are a mixture of bright and dark. The street was a quiet little enclave, a dead-end street with neat bungalows and lots of trees. Behind Lillie's house was the rear portion of the Central Baptist Church property, and right behind Lillie's yard, screened by a hedge, was a youth baseball field. In the summer, Lillie could sit on her porch and hear the birds singing and the breeze in the trees, and in the evenings, she could hear the laughter of children playing baseball. But I also remember her small living room. The focal point was a rocking chair, where Lillie would sit, quietly reading newspapers, magazines and books about mayhem and murder. I particularly remember a book about the recent capture of Adolph Eichmann, the Nazi responsible for the mass-murder of Jews.

Lillie eventually moved back to Mt. Vernon to be nearer her roots. In 1974 she had been suffering from dementia and was placed in a nursing home. She died in 1976 and is buried next to her beloved Noah in the Elmwood Cemetery in Mt. Vernon.

I regret not knowing Lillie better. In her later years, I was in college, and when she died I was in graduate school in another state. I was not able to attend her funeral. At the time, I was completely unaware of the events surrounding Noah's death. Noah had been her strength, but she had taken up his mantle of strength and wore it proudly.

Unlike the trajectory of Lillie's life, changed forever by Noah's murder, the course of Hunter Burchell's life appeared relatively unaltered by his actions and the events of early 1932. He had "dodged the bullet." He and his wife Ethel moved back to Clay County to be near his family, and he obtained a job with the State Highway Department building roads, no doubt aided by his family's influence.

For most of his life Hunter had been the younger brother supported by the rest of his family. They helped him land jobs and eventually funded his legal defense. They also paid for his defense in Lillie's 1935 lawsuit, and undoubtedly funded the $3,500 judgement.

However, influenced by his wife, Ethel, he was determined to become a better man and the course of his life gradually changed. He and Ethel raised a young Clay County girl named Ada Marie, he was able to hold down his job for years, he joined a church, mentored a nephew also named Hunter, and he eventually wrote Lillie a letter begging forgiveness. Did he write the letter solely at the urging of Ethel? Or did he lie awake at night, soaked in sweat and remorse, worrying about the pain he caused?

Jean Burchell told me that before she accidentally discovered Noah Tipton's death during her genealogy research, neither she nor any of the surviving Burchell family members had ever heard of Noah Tipton. The story of Hunter killing Noah Tipton had become a dark secret.

Hunter Burchell died on January 10, 1972 at the age of 76. His wife, Ethel, died in 1980, and they are both buried just outside of Manchester in the Burchell Cemetery near the hill where Hunter grew up.

Lillie Tipton's Letters to Ruby Laffoon and Replies

Mt. Vernon, KY — March 12, 1932
Governor Ruby Laffoon
Frankfort, KY

Dear Sir:

I write you in regard to the case of Commonwealth against Hunter Burchell, who was indicted in this Circuit Court for first degree murder in the killing of N.J. Tipton, my husband. After trial in Somerset, with the conviction of manslaughter, I have heard that an effort is being made to get executive clemency for him, and that there were many personal letters and interviews with you before and after the trial.

I want my friends to be heard before you consider this case. I know that my husband did not consider it a crime to call the Attorney General, about the way Hunter Burchell was taking care of the prisoner; neither did the women and men depositors of the bank closed wile F .E. Miller was cashier think that the warden had the right to allow the prisoner the liberty of the town; with no guard, when thus going over the town, with a citizen's coat, white shirt, and regular citizen's hat on, that he was here for three days to testify in cases in which the juries had not been selected, that it would take two days to try, and it would take only one and three-quarter hours to come from the reformatory. So these people repeatedly requested my husband to see if something could not be done, and these dissatisfied people said that the guard had been away from town for more than four hours and they thought that it was more of a vacation for the prisoner that his being brought here to testify in court.

This is the whole story up to the time that Burchell attacked him first and he, Burchell, brought on a second altercation at the time of the killing. See his testimony at the trial in Somerset. I want you to come, in person or in mind, and with my daughter, and two small granddaughters and myself, stand by the graves in our cemetery, where a grave, not sixty days old, holds the dearest part of my life; my protector from cold and hunger, my support in sickness, in health my companion at home and at church, my defender during the troubles of life, who was ruthlessly, wantonly and with malice taken from me. I want you to please think of this before you stretch forth your hand, clothed with the greatest power conferred on any man in this State, and cause the affixing of the seal of this Commonwealth as an approval of this wanton act of Hunter Burchell. Very respectfully. Mrs. N. J. Tipton

—⚬⚬—

April 11, 1932
Hon. Ruby Laffoon
Governor of Kentucky

Sir:

I have been informed that Hunter Burchell, convicted in the Pulaski Circuit Court, sentenced to serve two years in the State Penitentiary for the killing of my husband, N. J. Tipton, has applied for a pardon.

I would respectfully request that I be given a hearing when this case is brought before you for consideration.

Yours very respectfully,
Mrs. N.J. Tipton
Sheriff of Rockcastle County

—⚬⚬—

COMMONWEALTH OF KENTUCKY EXECUTIVE CHAMBER, FRANKFORT

April 14, 1932

Mrs. N. J. Tipton, Sheriff
Rockcastle County
Mt. Vernon, KY

Dear Mrs. Tipton
I have received your letter of April 11, addressed to the Governor, regarding Hunter Burchell, and have noted what you have to say regarding him.
In reply, will say in case a pardon is asked, you will be given a hearing before passing on same.

Yours very truly,
H. H. HOLMAN, Secretary to the Governor

—ɯ—

Hon. Ruby Laffoon
Governor of Kentucky

May 13, 1932

Sir:
I noticed in the papers you have granted a pardon to Hunter Burchell, convicted for the murder of my husband, N.J. Tipton. I was very much surprised, chagrined and humiliated when I ascertained your actions, in view of the fact that your secretary wrote me on the 14th day of April, 1932, in which he stated you would give me and my friends a hearing on my protest. From your reason as given in the papers, you granted this pardon on the testimony of two witnesses, who testified that my husband fired two shots be-

fore he was killed; one of these witnesses was successfully impeached on the trial of the case, and both witnesses who testified to this are indicted in the Rockcastle Circuit Court for perjury; each of them testified before the grand jury of Rockcastle and is now indicted for this perjured testimony.

There were a number of eyewitnesses to the killing, men, who no one can doubt their veracity, all of them who swore that my husband made no attempt to do this man any harm whatever, at the time he was shot and killed.

In your statement, you say from records before you, my husband was a fractious, high- tempered character and had previously killed other men. May I ask, from what source you received this information? There was not a line of evidence to this effect, introduced while in the trial of this case. The facts as to my husband killing other men—"While my husband was serving as Deputy Sheriff, he and Mr. J.C. Griffin, Sheriff of Rockcastle County were in discharge of their official duties in arresting two men, who when apprehended, opened fire on the officers, shooting the Sheriff down and dangerously shooting and wounding my husband; and in the fight that occurred, the two men were killed." The grand jury on three separate occasions, made a thorough investigation of this trouble, and on every occasion, exonerated my husband of any wrongdoing whatsoever, in the killing of these men. As to my husband's reputation for peace and law-abiding, there can not be a court record found in Kentucky, or any other State, where my husband was ever charged with violating the laws of the country in any respect. The facts as here given, are the reason his reputation for peace and quiet was not attacked in the trial of this case.

I am indeed surprised that the Governor of a great Commonwealth would be so biased and one-sided to refuse the family and 1,500 or more citizens who signed a petition requesting a hearing, and protesting a pardon in this case, a fair and impartial hearing..

God pity the law-abiding citizens of Kentucky, with the Chief Executive officer refusing to hear aggrieved citizens.

Believe me Sir,
Mrs. N. J. Tipton

Chapter Eleven

SUPPOSE, SUPPOSE

The iconic frontier lawman, Wyatt Earp, died on January 13th, 1929, almost three years to the day before Noah Tipton was killed. According to Earp biographer, Casey Tefertiller, as Earp lay on his death bed, he muttered his last words, "Suppose, suppose."

As the years rolled by, the Earp story grew, and many of the episodes of his life become part of the public vernacular. Who has not heard of the OK Corral? But, as Earp's reputation grew, so did the legend. Many authors and screen writers latched on to that legend and fictionalized his exploits, transforming a hard-nosed law enforcement officer into a mythic character with almost superhuman abilities. These writers have taken Wyatt's last words to heart. Suppose.

What if the story of Noah Tipton was fiction? How would a writer reconcile conflicting accounts of the shooting? I wrestled with the format for this book for years before deciding to simply lay out the story as a historical narrative, to let the evidence and record guide my hand. However, that decision came to me after I had written much of it as fiction. Early on, I also wrestled with the conflicting evidence as to whether Noah was able to draw his weapon and shoot, whether the event was a gunfight or an assassination. The following is my fictional conclusion to the story, a "last scene." Suppose....

—∽∾∾—

Mom sighed and stopped. She sat back in her chair, placed her coffee cup on the table, and folded her hands in her lap, as though she had reached some sort of closure. She paused for a few moments, removed her glasses and rubbed her eyes with her fingertips.

She began speaking, not much more than a whisper. "The newspapers reported that it started to rain, and that had he not been wearing his long overcoat, he could have gotten to his gun to defend himself. Of course, this is not what two of the witnesses said. They said he fired first. Burchell claimed to have fired in self-defense, but the prosecution witnesses, upstanding citizens, said it was not self-defense. This is something the jury could not reconcile."

"Noah was an expert shot. He had killed two men in the line of duty. If he had fired the first shot, or had he returned fire, the shots would have been at close range, and Burchell would have died. If he hadn't been able to retrieve his gun before he was shot, how in heaven's name did he draw his gun after being shot four times?"

She paused again, rubbing her hands. They were thin and delicate. I cleared my throat and waited. The grandfather clock in the hallway chimed.

Mom said slowly and patiently, "Go to my bedroom and look in the cedar chest and bring me the two boxes under the quilts."

I had earlier slipped off my boots, and I padded quietly over the hardwood floors in my sock-feet toward the bedroom. The floors creaked and I knew she was listening, knowing exactly where I was and whether I was going to the right place in the bedroom. I lifted the lid of the cedar chest and smelled the cedar and old fabric. I removed two big checkered quilts, one red and the other yellow, and placed them carefully on her bed. Lying at the bottom of the chest were two wooden boxes. I lifted them out, and one was heavier. I put the lighter box under my arm and carried them both back to the kitchen.

Mom had moved the dishes, leaving a space, and I placed the boxes side by side on the table. She slowly lifted opened the first box and removed a black felt hat. It was faded with age, and she held it to her face and breathed in.

"I can still smell his hair tonic, " she whispered.

I recognized the hat as the one Noah wore in his last photograph, where he had his arms around two little girls, Mom and Geri.

"He loved this hat," was all she said, as she placed it back in the box.

She opened the other box, the heavier one. She withdrew an object wrapped in oil cloth. She unwrapped it. The cloth was stiff with age, holding its creases. The cloth dropped onto the table, revealing a big revolver.

"The gun was with him when he died," she stated. "I don't like it, and never liked it in my house."

She placed the gun on the table and pushed it away. She reached back into the box and withdrew a long leather wallet. She opened it and held it out. An engraved silver and brass shield stared back at me.

"This is his badge. He took his job very seriously, like an honor, an obligation."

I rubbed it with my thumb and it brightened where I touched. She reached back into the box and lifted out a folded bundle. She set it on the table, gently patted it and rested her hands on it.

"All these years I've heard theories about the rain and why he didn't kill Burchell, and I've never said a word about the truth."

"What do you mean, the truth?" I asked.

"Noah was a kind and gentle man. He loved animals, his cat and his horse. He loved his family. He was a good father and a good husband, and he adored me and my sister.

But the truth of the matter was that he had a temper. Lillie called it his "panther". The two men he killed when he was a deputy probably needed killing, and someone would have probably killed them eventually. But Noah always felt like he killed them in the heat of the moment. It bothered him so much that he lay awake at night, worrying about whether he could have done this or that differently, whether he could have disarmed them without killing them."

I thought for a bit and asked, "So you are saying that he hesitated, that he could have defended himself but didn't because he was struggling with his temper?. Was that what got him killed? How can you know for sure? Maybe it *was* raining, and he really couldn't get to his gun before he was shot."

She thought for a few minutes and sighed. "I'm going to show you a secret that very few people have seen. This didn't come out in Burchell's trial. I am eighty-five years old, and this should not go to the grave with me."

She gently unfolded the bundle. It was a big woolen coat. It was gray, and had faint brown stains around two holes in the front.

"I tried to wash out the blood. Even cold water won't take out blood that has set for years."

"Are you telling me this is Noah's overcoat?

"Yes. My Daddy fetched it from the doctor, but he couldn't bear to give it to Lillie, with the blood and all. Momma tried to wash it and she gave it to me years later."

She turned in her chair and held out the coat and it unfolded, the bottom falling and draping in the floor. I looked closely at it. It was musty and had some moth damage, but I could tell it had once been a fine coat.

Mom turned it and folded it carefully in her lap, one sleeve facing up. "See?"

I scooted my chair closer and examined the coat. It looked completely normal. There was a pocket with a button on it.

I imagined him standing in the cold, his hands in the pockets, squinting into the rain, not expecting the shots.

Mom then lifted the coat and turned it over. The other side, Noah's right side, appeared identical to the left. Then she lifted the sleeve. Unlike the other side, there was a long hemmed slit, from the pocket to the bottom of the coat. I looked at Mom.

"What is that?" I asked.

"Do you remember me telling you how he loved me, my good grades, my piano playing, my sewing? I would sew buttons on his shirts, hem his trousers. Back in those days, little girls learned to do things like that at a very young age. I altered this coat for him."

"Afterward I didn't think much about it. I was so young. I eventually forgot. But when Momma gave me his coat and these things before she died, I saw the coat and remembered."

I sat, stunned. Had Noah somehow had a feeling, a premonition, that he might need to get to his gun quickly? It made perfect sense. Kentucky winters are cold and rainy. But why had he not defended himself? He had a run-in with Burchell that morning and townsfolk had told him Burchell was going around bragging he would kill him. Why hadn't he defended himself?

"Mom, if he could have drawn his gun, why didn't he?"

"I believe he did. I will believe to my dying day that when he saw Burchell draw a gun, he drew his own gun, but tried to keep hold of his temper, thinking he might talk Burchell into a peaceful ending. He tried to keep the panther caged..."

Her eyes moistened and her voice trembled as she finished, ".....and it got him killed."

She paused and took a deep breath, and almost as a footnote said, "The conflicting stories bothered me for years. In my dreams I was haunted by the gunshots. Not just the four that killed Pa Tipton. I hear five shots. That last shot was fired by Deputy Carter as he struggled with Burchell, as Pa lay dying in the street."

She paused again and began folding the coat and said, "That last shot, not fired by Pa in anger, but by Deputy Carter, confused everyone...the people who heard the shots, the witnesses, and even the jury. That confusion got Burchell a shamefully light jail sentence, and eventually a pardon."

Mom looked at me and said. "In his last moments, Noah tried to do the right thing. He could have killed Hunter Burchell, but he didn't. We should all be so good."

—◆—

Most good stories have a story arc, a theme, or a tragic flaw that is illustrated by the journey of its protagonist. Mom once told me that Noah was a "hard man." In a literary sense, Noah was a hero...an Odysseus or Beowulf or Hamlet, a man who had faced slings and arrows. And like Odysseus, he had faced monsters. But Noah's journey became a tragedy. Did he have a tragic flaw that culminated in his own death?

I now believe that journey may also be my journey. There was absolutely no logical reason, no moral excuse, that Hunter Burchell had to kill Noah Tipton. In 1932, men who did not waiver in their enforcement of the law were necessary and appreciated. However, I have now come to realize that perhaps Noah did contribute to his own death by being such a hard man.

I once had a co-worker tell me that I had a killer instinct. At the time I was in charge of all of the human resource matters for an organization with two-hundred full-time employees and over five hundred seasonal workers. I like to think that I approached issues like discipline with a sense of humanity, but, in the interest of the organization and its mission, I probably did not exhibit a lot of patience. You misbehave, you pay the price.

In the years since Mom's death I have looked to Noah to help me keep my panther caged. Sometimes it gets out, and sometimes it doesn't. But I see Noah and hear Mom's words when the beast is clawing at the door.

Chapter Twelve
GOD'S AIR

On the last trip I took with Mom to discover the world of Noah Tipton, we visited the cemetery where Noah and Lillie are buried. We carried with us an old photograph of Noah's funeral. In it there are well dressed women and farmers and businessmen standing around Noah's casket at the cemetery. There are also several young boys wearing leather aviator hats, a trend started by Charles Lindbergh, one that continued after Amelia Earhart made her transatlantic flight. Even in an age when people could take wing on complicated machines and fly, sheriffs were still being shot down in the street.

In the photo, there was a spindly sapling growing in the background. I held up the old photo and asked Mom to move left a bit so I could take a photo of her from the same angle. She was uncomfortable and fidgeted. The tree, much larger now, formed a backdrop to this drama. I snapped the picture and captured the scene.

Standing next to Noah's and Lillie's graves, I looked down at the spring grass, knowing that Noah, not the story, but the actual Noah Tipton, was only six feet—seventy-two inches—below my feet. I wondered if I should put my ear to the cold ground and listen to the real story. If six feet of dirt did not separate us could I reach down and touch his hand and feel the panic and wide-eyed realization that he must have felt as he lay on the street dying?

On the drive home, Mom sat silently. I knew that seeing the graves of those she had loved and lost made her sad.

She finally sighed and said, "It was a cold day. We were family, so we sat in front on chairs in the grass. Everyone else stood behind us. I sat in Daddy's lap and he opened up his coat and pulled it around me to keep me warm. Geri sat in Momma's lap."

She paused again, looking out the car window as the houses gave way to farmhouses and then to just farmland. She opened her purse to find something, but closed it instead. She sighed again.

"I don't remember what was said, but a lot of people were crying. I didn't cry but I felt like I should." She opened her purse again and removed a tissue.

"The little road that circles the cemetery was jammed with cars. We had to wait a long time to leave. I didn't cry, but I should have."

Mom paused for a long time. I thought I should say something, anything.

She finally asked, "Why did those things happen?"

It occurred to me that maybe God doesn't create tragedy, but that He does give us the strength to endure it. I didn't want to question Mom's belief in an omnipotent God, so I simply replied, "I don't know."

This was our last trip together. Mom had COPD and it was difficult and embarrassing for her to travel carrying oxygen tanks. Chronic Obstructive Pulmonary Disease is a horrible fiend. Slowly, and over several years, it becomes more and more difficult for a victim to breathe. They say it is like drowning, only slower.

It took ten years for the fiend to finally take my mother. It was nothing she did. My father had been a heavy smoker, so maybe it was secondhand smoke. Or maybe it was growing up in an environment hazy with smoke from wood fireplaces and coal furnaces. The last few years she was burdened by various tanks and hoses and machines, some portable and some the size of heavy luggage, upon which she depended to live. Other than the normal frailty of a woman in her eighties, she was in good health. Except for her lungs.

We were constantly terrified she would catch a cold or the sniffles, ailments that a younger or healthier person could casually endure. She finally did.

I was sitting in her bedroom helping her with her income taxes. She had an accountant, but, was still required to assemble receipts and check stubs and the like.

"Did you find the receipt for your shirt?", she asked for the third time. "Yes, Mom!" I was tired and a bit short with her.

She had ordered me a shirt for my birthday from Cabela's and she was one of the one percent of the taxpayers who actually reported the purchases so she could pay the state-mandated, but usually ignored sales tax on mail-order sales. She sneezed and said that her throat was scratchy.

The next morning, a nurse called and said Mom had been transported to the local emergency room. The following days were a nightmare. Mom weakened, and we were advised to consider a DNR. "Do not resuscitate."

On the third day I called a palliative care physician and explained Mom's situation. Mom was wearing a mask that forced air into her lungs. She was not lucid, and she was being fed through an I.V.

"How do you know when to let her go?" I tearfully asked.

"Bring in her grandchildren. If she smiles and responds, then there is a spark, a love of life. If not, you will know if she's ready to go."

"If she is ready, then what do we do?"

"Just let her breathe God's air."

It is easy to take air for granted. My life endeavors have led me to a unique appreciation for air. Mom used to tell me, as a toddler, I loved chasing bubbles on the breeze. I was a lifeguard in my youth and learned the mechanics of breathing life into a drowning victim. I raced bicycles and learned to appreciate the subtleties of drafting in the peloton to overcome wind resistance. I have been an avid bowhunter for over fifty years, and the wind can be a bowhunter's worst enemy or best friend. I love to inhale the Kentucky autumn breezes.

As we sat weeping, watching Mom fade away, I thought of Noah. An assassin's bullet had taken his air, and now my mother, the last witness to Noah's story, was breathing God's air for the last time.

We had a very nice funeral for Mom. She had many friends who attended. The Church was packed, and my kids sang a hymn.

If this story had been a novel, Mom would have solved the mystery before she died. She would have remembered a forgotten detail that would explain whether Noah did or did not draw his weapon before the gunshots rang out in the January twilight. But this is not a novel. All we can do is speculate. All we know for sure is that Burchell simply got the drop on Noah and killed him.

It has been ten years, but I still visit Mom's grave regularly. I rotate seasonal flowers and keep the crabgrass from creeping across her footstone. I am grateful for the chance that Noah gave me to be a better son. Mom was the window to Noah's story, but he had been my window to the heart of my mother.

Epilogue

The American Justice System, the same system that Sheriffs Noah and Lillie Tipton had sworn to uphold and had risked their lives for, failed them.

Each year, thousands of executive pardons are granted for convicted felons. While less common, pardoning killers still occurs. In 2019, in a Pulitzer Prize-winning story, the *Louisville Courier Journal* reported that Kentucky's outgoing governor pardoned a felon convicted of killing an occupant during a home invasion. The story also reported that the killer's brother had hosted a fundraiser for the governor.

Sources

Cover
Donna McKnight concept design
Photo—Wathalyne Carman Hendrick collection

Prologue
Lexington Leader (Lexington, KY) 1/18/32
Jean Burchell
Kentucky State Archives, Frankfort, KY Mark Morgan

Chapter 1- The Memorial
Elaine Carman recollections
Kentucky Law Enforcement Memorial Foundation, Wathalyne Carman Hendrick recollections Wathalyne Carman Hendrick photo collection

Chapter 2- January 16, 1932
Burchell, Bea-photo collection
Burchell, Jean
Commonwealth Journal (Somerset, KY) 1/20/32, 3/2/32, 3/9/32
Courier Journal (Louisville, KY) 1/17/32, 3/3/32, 3/4/32
Hopkins, Kenneth interview 2016
Kentucky Advocate (Danville, KY) 1/18/32
Lexington Leader (Lexington, KY) 1/18/32
Mt. Vernon Signal, 1/20/32
Pennington, Dr. Monroe-Noah Tipton Death Certificate
Peters, Mike—Rockcastle County Sheriff, 2018 interview

Smith, Jerri Lynn Nunnelley recollections
Wathalyne Carman Hendrick photo collection
Wathalyne Carman Hendrick recollections
Sedalia Democrat (Sedalia, MO) 1/17/32

Chapter 3- Troubling Times
Benson, Lula and Dora Fleck, *Butch Cassidy, My Brother*,
    BYU Press 1975
Eichengreen, Barry; (1992) *Golden Fetters: The Gold Standard & the Great Depression*
Jean Burchell
Gorn, Elliott J., *Dillinger's Wild Ride*, 2009
Guinn, Jeff, *Go Down Together, True Story of Bonnie & Clyde*, Simon & Schuster 2010
Lake, Stuart, *Wyatt Earp-Frontier Marshal*, Houghton-Mifflin, NY 1931
McCarty, Lea Franklin, *The Gunfighters*, 1959
Parker, Randall, *Reflections on the Great Depression*, Elgar Publishing 2003
Pearce, John Ed, *Days of Darkness-The Feuds of Eastern Kentucky*, University Press of Kentucky, 1994
Remember When (1932) , Seek Publishing (pamphlet)
Tefertiller, Casey, *Wyatt Earp-The Life Behind the Legend*, John Wiley and Sons, 1997
Urschel, Joe, *The Year of Fear*, St. Martin's Press, 2015
Worster, Donald, *Dust Bowl: The Southern Plains in the 1930's*, Oxford University Press, New York, 2004

Chapter 4- Mt. Vernon
Author's recollections
Hardin, Bayless "*Early Trails and Roads Through the Wilderness of Southeastern Kentucky*" (map) 1948
"Find a County", National Association of Counties, 2011
Historical Census Browser, University of Virginia Library, 2014

Leip, David, "Dave Leip's Atlas of U.S .Presidential Elections", 2018

McKnight, Donna, Downtown Map using Google Maps

McKnight, Donna, Kentucky Map

Renner, Jeff, *Three Springs and a Wilderness Station*, 2013

Smith, Jerri Lynn Nunnelley recollections

Tatum, Lynn- interview 2020

U.S. Census Bureau 1900-1990 "Population of Counties by Decennial Census"

Chapter 5- Noah and Lillie

Advocate Messenger (Danville, KY) 1/19/32

Ancestry Sources for the Tipton and Roark Family Trees, including notes.

12th Census of the U.S.-Harlan County District 53

14th Census of the U.S.-Rockcastle County-District 235

15th Census of the U.S.-Rockcastle County-District 13

Carman, William F. – Anestry.com DNA Analysis

Courier Journal (Louisville, KY) 1/19/32

Ehle, John, *Trail of Tears: Rise & Fall of the Cherokee Nation*, Knopf—Doubleday, 2011

Jean Burchell

Harlan County Marriage Records-1903

Interior Journal (Stanford, KY) 6/5/28, 8/6/29, 2/25/30, 1/22/32

Kennedy, Brent, *The Melungeons—The Resurrection of a Proud People*, Mercer

University Press 1997

Kentucky Atlas and Gazetteer—DeLorme map book 2001

Lucille and Preston Nunnelley recollections

Madison County Births—1904 (Courthouse Records) New York Times (New York, NY) 8/15/36

Pearl Carter Pace Collection 1902-2000, Western Kentucky University Library Special Collections

Rockcastle County Court Orders p.357, 1/20/1932

Wathalyne Hendrick Carman photo collection

Wathalyne Carman Hendrick recollections

Wathalyne Carman Hendrick handwritten family tree

Hopkins, Kenneth interview 2016

Oplinger, Randy, Recollections and Helton Family Research

Peters, Mike-Rockcastle County Sheriff-2018 interview

Roark, Clifford Dewey- Recollections and Helton family research

Smith, Jerri Lynn Nunnelley recollections

Tipton, Noah-Draft Registration Card, 1915

Ehle, John, *Trail of Tears:The Rise and Fall of the Cherokee Nation*, Knopf—Doubleday 2011

Wallis, Michael, *David Crockett: The Lion of the West,* WW Norton and Co. NY 2011

Chapter 6- *The 1927 Gunfight*

Advocate Messenger (Danville, KY) 1/18/32

Courier Journal (Louisville, KY) 5/16/32

Ellison, Betty, *Illegal Odyssey: 200 Years of Kentucky Moonshine*, Author House 2003

Farris, Gus—West Virginia, Interview 2021

"History of Stock Car Racing", Belk Library, Appalachian State University 2015

Indianapolis News (Indianapolis, IN) 1/18/32

Interior Journal (Stanford, KY) 11/16/27

Interview with Kenneth Hopkins 2016

Iorizzo, Luciano, *Al Capone, A Biography*, Greenwood Publishing, 2003

Jean Burchell

Kellner, Esther, *Moonshine: Its History and Folklore*, Bobbs—Merrill 1971

Kentucky Atlas and Gazetteer—DeLorme mao book, 2001

Mt. Vernon Signal newspaper, 1/26/1917

McGirr,Lisa, *The War on Alcohol: Prohibition and the Rise of the American State*, WW Norton Co. 2016

"Organized Crime-American Mafia", American Law and
Legal Information
Photos and Recollections by Author
Tipton, Lillie- Letters to Laffoon-(Louisville) Courier Jour-
nal-5/16/32

Chapter 7- *Hunter Burchell*

Advocate Messenger (Danville, KY) 1/18/32, 1/19/32,
1.23/32, 3/5/32, 4/21/32, 5/13/32, 5/14/32
Kentucky Advocate (Danville, KY) 1/18/32, 2/2/32, 3/2/32,
3/3/32, 3/7/32, 5/11/32, 1/19/34
Bea Burchell photo collection
Jean Burchell
Robert S. Burchell recollections
Caron's City Directory, Frankfort, KY 1932
Clay County Ancestral News magazine (Vol.25 No.2)
Clay County Genealogy and Historical Society-Manchester, KY
Courier Journal (Louisville, KY) 1/17/22, 10/1/31, 1/17/32,
2/26/32, 3/2/32, 3/3/32, 3/6/32, 3/24/32, 4/20/32, 4/30/32,
5/12/32, 5/13/32, 5/14/32.
Federal Census Report, Manchester, Clay County, KY 1900,
1910, 1920, 1930, 1940
Indianapolis News (Indianapolis, IN) 1/18/32
Interior Journal (Stanford, KY) 11/23/34, 1/22/35
Kentucky Advocate (Danville, KY) 1/18/32
Mountain Advocate (Barbourville, KY) 9/23/21
Ralph and Catherine Hollin, *Greenbriar Memories*
Sedalia Democrat (Sedalia, MO) 1/17/32
U.S. Army Transport Service, Passenger Lists,1910-1931

Chapter 8- *Noah's Gun*

"1860 Henry" (pamphlet) Fort Smith National Historic Site,
National Park Service
Adler, Dennis—"Killing the Old West", *Guns of the Wild
West Magazine*, Winter 2019

Boorman, Dean K, *The History of Smith and Wesson Firearms*, Lyons Press, 2002

Interior Journal (Stanford, KY) 11/16/27, 6/3/32

Laffoon, Ruby, Executive Order to Pardon Hunter Burchell 5/9/32

Photos of guns and badge by author

Preston and Lucille Nunnelley

"Killing Bill Tilghman" — *True West Magazine* 7/2014

Jean Burchell

Pennington, Dr. Monroe, Noah Tipton's Death Certificate

Schreier, Phillip, "Guaranteed by Us—The Winchester Model 1873", *American Rifleman Magazine*, NRA, Vol.161-#11, 11/13

Tipton, Lillie, Letters to Ruby Laffoon, (from *Louisville Courier Journal*) 5/16/32

Rockcastle County Sheriff Mike Peters interview—2018

Trimble, Marshall- Arizona State Historian

Zou, Youyou, Quartz News, 10/16/17

Chapter 9- The Trial

Commonwealth Journal (Somerset, KY) 1/20/32, 1/27/32, 3/2/32, 3/9/32

Courier Journal (Louisville, KY) 1/17/32, 1/18/32, 3/2/32, 3/3/32, 3/4/32, 3/6/32, 3/24/32, 4/20/32, 4/30/32, 5/12/32, 5/16/32, 11/22/32

Indianapolis News (Indianapolis, IN) 1/18/32

Interior Journal (Stanford, KY) 2/27/31, 11/22/35, 11/26/35

Kentucky Advocate (Danville, KY) 1/18/32, 1/25/32, 1/27/32, 2/19/32, 3/2/32, 3/7/32, 4/21/32, 5/5/32, 5/11/32

Laffoon, Ruby, Executive Order to Pardon Hunter Burchell 5/13/32

Mt. Vernon Signal (Mt. Vernon, KY) 1/21/32

Pennington, Monroe, Noah Tipton Death Certificate

Rockcastle County Heritage Committee, *Rockcastle County and Its People* 2010

Rockcastle Circuit Court-Motion for Hunter Burchell's bail (undated)

1/19/32—Rockcastle Circuit Court-Petition for Change in Venue

1/19/32—Rockcastle Circuit Court-Objection to Change in Venue

1/19/32—Rockcastle Circuit Court- Affidavits (14 signers) in favor of Change in Venue

1/20/32—Rockcastle Circuit Court- Affidavits (9 signers) against Change in Venue (undated)—Rockcastle Circuit Court-Motion to Require Judge Tarter to Vacate Bench (undated)—Rockcastle Circuit Court-(Bunch) Affidavit in favor of motion-Tarter to vacate

1/20/32—Rockcastle Circuit Court-Response to Petition for Change in Venue

Tarter, Jury Instructions-Pulaski Circuit Court 3/5/32

W. Daniel Carman, interview by author

Wathalyne Carman Hendrick recollections

Chapter 10- Aftermath

5/7/32—Pulaski Circuit Court-Order for Vincent Wesley to transcribe proceedings.

5/9/32—Pulaski Circuit Court-Denial of Forma Pauperis Request.

Caudill, Harry, *Night Comes to the Cumberlands, (1963) Jesse Stuart Foundation 2001*

Commonwealth Journal (Somerset, KY) 3/9/31

Gipson, Vernon, *Ruby Laffoon, Governor of Kentucky 1931-1935*, Earlington, KY

Hopkins, Kenneth interview 2016

Interior Journal (Stanford, KY), 8/3/32

Jillson, Willard, *Governor Ruby Laffoon, A Sketch*, Kentucky Historical Society, 1932

Laffoon, Ruby, Executive Order to Pardon Hunter Burchell, 5/13/32

Tipton, Lillie, Letters to Ruby Laffoon, (from Louisville Courier Journal) 5/16/32 (undated)—Pulaski Circuit Court-Motion for New Trial

(undated)—Pulaski Circuit Court-Motion of Appeal-Forma Pauperis

Chapter 11- *Suppose Suppose*
Casey Tefertiller, *Wyatt Earp-The Life Behind the Legend*
Wathalyne Carman Hendrick recollections

Chapter 12- *God's Air*
Photo from Wathalyne Carman Hendrick collection
Photo by author

Epilogue
Courier Journal (Louisville, KY), 12/11/2019

ACKNOWLEDGMENTS

This book, from my first hearing the story, until publication, took nearly forty years to write. During that time, I have spoken with so many people and visited so many places important to the story that it is almost impossible to remember them all. This modest acknowledgment is an attempt to express my appreciation to those that contributed.

Jean Burchell, and her generosity, have been critical to my research. I appreciate the hospitality of Preston and Lucille Nunnelley, who were Lillie Tipton's caregivers and the repository for many of her keepsakes. Jerri Lynn and Keith Smith, who still live in Mt. Vernon, have been so gracious and helpful. My brother, John Carman, and his wife Elaine have been supportive, and Elaine accompanied Mom to memorial ceremony at the opening of this book. The Helton family, and its patriarch, Kenneth Hopkins have contributed much generosity and information. My friend and co-worker, the late Mark Morgan, graciously started me on my research. My son, Dan Carman, and his father-in-law, Judge Bruce Butler, have provided me with much legal insight.

I would be remiss if I didn't thank Lissa Archer and the folks at Lynn Imaging in Lexington, who I kept busy scanning and emailing documents. Lynn Tatum with Rockcastle County Tourism was a valuable source of Mt. Vernon history. Donna McKnight shared her graphic arts talent in the maps and cover layout. My West Virginia friend, Gus Farris, gave me valuable insight into the world of moonshining. Thanks to Former Rockcastle County Sheriff Mike Peters who provided me with much needed insight into the workings of his department. Mike also initiated Noah Tipton's nomination to the Kentucky Law Enforcement Memorial.

Lt. Col. Tom Pyzic gave me the perspective of an officer facing an angry man. The staffs at the Kentucky State Archives, the University of Kentucky King Library, the Rockcastle County Library, the Pulaski County Library, and the Clay County Library were courteous, thoughtful, and hardworking.

Of course, my wife Maureen deserves a big thanks for patiently listening to the ramblings of an author in over his head. Maureen was an English teacher and lawyer, and has kept me headed in the right direction, both in this endeavor, and in life.

And last, I would like to express my love and appreciation to my late mother, without whom this book would not have been started or finished. She was my friend.

About the Author

Bill Carman is a hunting and fishing guide and successful outdoor writer. His stories have appeared in *Traditional Bowhunter Magazine, Primitive Archer, TradArchers' World, Bugle Magazine,* and *Lexington Family.* He won the national Outdoor Life Book Club Short Story contest and has written three books of hunting and fishing essays.

Saving Noah is his first venture into the true crime genre. He and his wife live in Lexington, Kentucky, where he is teaching his grandchildren the ways of the woods. Bill can be reached at *www.kentuckywildoutdoors.com.*

Index

Goebel, William 55

Griffin, John 22, 23, 24, 34, 44, 45, 48, 49, 50, 51, 52, 53, 57, 64, 69, 95, 103, 104, 105, 113, 114, 119, 127, 132

H

Haff, R.C. 56

Hauptmann, Bruno Richard 101

Hazard Herald 121

Helton, Jerusha Ledford 36

Helton, John Shade 36

Helton, Lillie 28, 41

Hendrick, Bill 15

Hendrick, Wathalyne Tipton Fairchild Carman 8, 15, 16, 45, 66, 67

Hensley, Jane 42

Hensley, Martha Patsey 37, 41

Hensley, Samuel 37, 42

Holman, H.H. 120, 131

Hopkins, Kenneth 107, 124, 125, 154

I

Irvin, TB 41

J

Jackson, Andrew 40

K

Kelly, George (Machine Gun) 27, 126

Kentucky Law Enforcement Memorial Foundation 15

L

Laffoon, Ruby 52, 91, 106, 118, 120, 122, 123, 129, 130

Lake, Stuart 27

Langford, Stephen 30

Ledford, William 41

Lewis, Sam 124

Lexington, Kentucky 127

Lexington Leader 8

Lindbergh, Anne Morrow 101

Lindbergh, Charles 27, 101, 102, 141

Lindbergh, Jr., Charles 101

Louisville Courier Journal 120, 145

Lynn, Wiley 63

M

Manchester, Kentucky 31, 54, 108, 124

Manning, Judge 124

Masterson, Bat 63

McKnight, Donna 154

Miller, Floyd 19, 27, 56, 57, 103, 104, 109, 112, 129

Miller, Robert 19, 27, 56, 103

Morgan, Mark 8, 154

Mt. Vernon, Kentucky 16, 23, 28, 30, 32, 44, 45, 53, 56, 57, 70, 99, 124, 127

Mullins, Bentley 53, 126

Mullins, Cam 49, 50, 51, 53, 64

Mullins, Dolora 126

Mullins Station, Kentucky 48, 49, 64

Murrell, L.V. 106, 107

N

National Prohibition Act 47

Nelson, Baby Face 27

Ness, Elliott 27

Nunnelley, Geraldine 126

Nunnelley, Lucille 59, 127, 154

Nunnelley, Preston 127, 154

Nunnelley, Sr., Preston 59, 73, 126

P

Pace, Pearl Carter 124

Paint Lick, Kentucky 42, 43, 44

Parker, Bonnie 26, 126

See More Great Books
at
WWW.ACCLAIMPRESS.COM

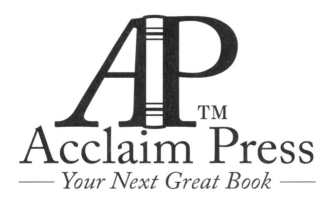